Lecture Notes in Computer Science　　9657

Commenced Publication in 1973
Founding and Former Series Editors:
Gerhard Goos, Juris Hartmanis, and Jan van Leeuwen

More information about this series at http://www.springer.com/series/7412

Bart Lamiroy · Rafael Dueire Lins (Eds.)

Graphic Recognition

Current Trends and Challenges

11th International Workshop, GREC 2015
Nancy, France, August 22–23, 2015
Revised Selected Papers

 Springer

Editors
Bart Lamiroy
Université de Lorraine
Vandoeuvre-lès-Nancy
France

Rafael Dueire Lins
Universidade Federal de Pernambuco
Recife, Pernambuco
Brazil

ISSN 0302-9743   ISSN 1611-3349   (electronic)
Lecture Notes in Computer Science
ISBN 978-3-319-52158-9   ISBN 978-3-319-52159-6   (eBook)
DOI 10.1007/978-3-319-52159-6

Library of Congress Control Number: 2016962025

LNCS Sublibrary: SL6 – Image Processing, Computer Vision, Pattern Recognition, and Graphics

Printed on acid-free paper

This Springer imprint is published by Springer Nature
The registered company is Springer International Publishing AG
The registered company address is: Gewerbestrasse 11, 6330 Cham, Switzerland

Preface

As for all previous editions, the 11th International Workshop on Graphics Recognition (GREC 2015) was organized by IAPR TC-10. The workshop, which was held August 22–23, 2015, took place in Nancy, France, after having been preventively relocated twice, following the Bardo and Sousse terrorist attack at the originally planned locations in Tunisia. It is extremely regretful that the initial chosen locations for GREC 2015 had to be cancelled for safety reasons, following the tragic terrorist strikes there. We warmly extend our sympathy and support to the Tunisian people and especially to our Tunisian colleagues who actively supported and contributed to the relocation in Nancy, France, notwithstanding all efforts made for a successful event in Tunis. We sincerely hope GREC will be held in Tunisia in the near future. Although GREC in Nancy was a success, subsequent events have unfortunately shown that relocating to France could have been just as dreadful.

GREC is organized every two years, in close conjunction with ICDAR, and aims at providing a unique atmosphere, fostering a very high level of interaction, discussion, and exchange of ideas (distinctly different from classic conference-like presentations) while providing high-quality and good-impact post-proceedings. It therefore represents an excellent opportunity for researchers and practitioners at all levels of experience to meet colleagues and to share new ideas and knowledge about graphics recognition methods. Graphics recognition is a subfield of document image analysis that deals with graphical entities in written documents, engineering drawings, maps, architectural plans, musical scores, mathematical notation, tables, diagrams, etc.

GREC 2015 has continued the tradition of past workshops held at Penn State University (USA, 1995), Nancy (France, 1997), Jaipur (India, 1999), Kingston (Canada, 2001), Barcelona (Spain, 2003), Hong Kong (China, 2005), Curitiba (Brazil, 2007), La Rochelle (France, 2009), Seoul (South Korea, 2011), and Lehigh University (USA, 2013).

With this edition, once again, the GREC workshops have proven to live up to the series expectations: The level of interaction was intense and rich, despite the sad context of the relocation.

The program was, as usual, organized in a single-track two-day workshop. It comprised several sessions dedicated to specific topics related to graphics in document analysis and graphic recognition. Each session began with an introductory talk by the session chairs, describing the state of the art, putting the presented talks in a more global perspective, and stating the current open challenges of session topics. This introduction was then followed by a number of short talks presenting solutions to some of these questions or presenting results of the speaker's work. Each session was concluded by a panel discussion.

For this edition, the program consisted of 19 scientific presentations and one contest report. It contained both classic and emerging topics of graphics recognition. Session topics included symbol spotting, recognition in context, perceptual-based approaches and grouping, low-level processing, off-line to on-line and interactive systems, structure-based approaches, performance evaluation and ground truthing, and content-based retrieval.

We would like to thank the SAGE research group in Sousse, for their initial commitment, strong contributions, and their kind help transferring the event to Tunis: Amira Bacha, Anis Kricha, Bassem Seddik, Hédi Yazid, Imen Abroug Abdelghani, Karim Kalti, Khawla Jayech, Mohamed Ali Mahjoub, Mohamed Aymen Charrada, Mohamed Neji Maâtouk, Ramzi Chaieb, and Sami Gazzah.

The current post-proceedings contain the reviewed and extended versions of ten selected works presented at the workshop.

Enjoy!

December 2016   Rafael Dueire Lins
                                                                    Bart Lamiroy

Organization

General Chairs

Najoua Essoukri Ben Amara   ENISO, SAGE Unit, Tunisia
Jean-Marc Ogier   Université de la Rochelle, L3i, France

Program Chairs

Bart Lamiroy   Université de Lorraine, Loria (UMR 7503), France
Rafael Dueire Lins   Federal University of Pernambuco, Brazil
Prasenjit Mitra   Penn State University, USA

TC-10 Steering Committee

Jean-Christophe Burie   Université de la Rochelle, France
Alicia Fornès   Universitat Autònoma de Barcelona, Spain
Bart Lamiroy   Université de Lorraine, France
Rafael Lins   Federal University of Pernambuco, Brazil
Josep Llados   Universitat Autònoma de Barcelona, Spain
Jean-Marc Ogier   Université de la Rochelle, France

Program Committee

Sébastien Adam	France
Gady Agam	USA
Luc Brun	France
Syed Saqib Bukhari	Germany
Jean-Christophe Burie	France
Pedro Company	Spain
Bertrand Coüasnon	France
Mickaël Coustaty	France
Vincenzo Deufemia	Italy
Alicia Fornés	Spain
Xiaoyi Jiang	Germany
Afef Kacem	Tunisia
Wenyin Liu	China
Josep Llados	Spain
Tong Lu	China
Muhammad Muzzamil Luqman	France
Mohamed Ali Mahjoub	Tunisia

Contents

Performance Analysis and Ground Truth

Circle Detection Performance Evaluation Revisited   3
   Elisa H. Barney Smith and Bart Lamiroy

The Creation of Synthetic Digital Ground-Truth Images of Historic
Cosmic Ray Data Recordings   19
   Vincent Mattana, Günther Drevin, and Pierre Roux

Statistical Performance Metrics for Use with Imprecise Ground-Truth   31
   Bart Lamiroy and Pascal Pierrot

Recognition and Content Analysis

Migrating the Classical Pen-and-Paper Based Conceptual Sketching
of Architecture Plans Towards Computer Tools - Prototype Design
and Evaluation   47
   Johannes Bayer, Syed Saqib Bukhari, Christoph Langenhan,
   Marcus Liwicki, Klaus-Dieter Althoff, Frank Petzold,
   and Andreas Dengel

Recognizing Electronic Circuits to Enrich Web Documents
for Electronic Simulation   60
   Shubham Agarwal, Mohit Agrawal, and Santanu Chaudhury

Ontology-Based Understanding of Architectural Drawings   75
   Lluís-Pere de las Heras, Oriol Ramos Terrades, and Josep Lladós

A System for Camera-Based Retrieval of Heterogeneous-Content Complex
Linguistic Map   86
   Bao Quoc Dang, Phuong Le Viet, Muhammad Muzzamil Luqman,
   Mickael Coustaty, De Tran Cao, and Jean-Marc Ogier

Low Level, Segmentation and Structured Data

Towards the Alignment of Handwritten Music Scores   103
   Pau Riba, Alicia Fornés, and Josep Lladós

Improving Fuzzy Multilevel Graph Embedding Technique by Employing
Topological Node Features: An Application to Graphics Recognition   117
   Hana Jarraya, Muhammad Muzzamil Luqman, and Jean-Yves Ramel

Text-Independent Speech Balloon Segmentation for Comics and Manga   133
   Christophe Rigaud, Jean-Christophe Burie, and Jean-Marc Ogier

Author Index   149

Performance Analysis and Ground Truth

Circle Detection Performance
Evaluation Revisited

Elisa H. Barney Smith[1] and Bart Lamiroy[2(✉)]

[1] Electrical and Computer Engineering Department, Boise State University,
Boise, ID 83725-2075, USA
ebarneysmith@boisestate.edu
[2] Université de Lorraine – Loria (UMR 7503),
Campus Scientifique – BP 239, 54506 Vandœuvre-lès-Nancy Cedex, France
bart.lamiroy@loria.fr

Abstract. Circle and circular arc detection in images have been a long
standing topic in image analysis. It finds numerous applications for both
scanned document images as well as in photographic images. As a result,
circle detection algorithms are published regularly and benchmarking
data sets and contests have been organized on a regular basis over the
last decades. Unfortunately, they have not been able to achieve a very
clear image establishing which approaches perform best and under what
exact conditions.

This paper contributes to circle and arc detection, by providing an
open and fully reproducible framework for benchmarking and evaluating circle and circular arc detection methods. It builds upon the current
state of the art and commonly used metrics by providing a complementary approach through the introduction of synthetic evaluation data for
benchmarking versus two noise types at gradually varying noise levels
and new performance metrics that are compatible with previous evaluation approaches.

1 Introduction

Circle and arc detection have been a long standing challenge in the Graphics
Recognition community [18] and beyond. New algorithms and approaches are
still being published on a regular basis without there being a clear knowledge of
their actual performance with respect to the state-of-the-art. This paper is an
attempt to provide an overview of past performance evaluation and benchmarking initiatives, and to initiate a more reproducible and complete way of assessing
circle and arc detection methods.

1.1 GREC Arc Detection Contests

The most consistent and complete series of benchmarking initiatives are the
Circle and Arc Detection Contests that have been held in conjunction with the
IAPR Graphics Recognition Workshops (GREC). These events have been taken

© Springer International Publishing AG 2017
B. Lamiroy and R. Dueire Lins (Eds.): GREC 2015, LNCS 9657, pp. 3–18, 2017.
DOI: 10.1007/978-3-319-52159-6_1

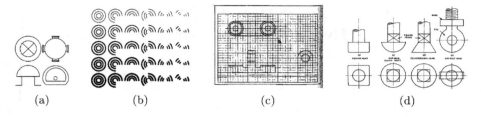

(a)   (b)   (c)   (d)

Fig. 1. Samples from GREC circle and arc detection contests (a) 2003 (b) 2005 (c) 2007 (d) 2009.

place every other year, and between 2001 and 2013, seven contests have been organised: [4, 5, 7, 15, 16, 18, 23].

For the purpose of objective benchmarking, each of these contests have contributed to providing annotated reference data. These either consist of synthetic data subjected to noise models, or of actually manually annotated scanned documents. The images are sometimes simple circles or parts of circles that do not touch, circles in patterns deliberately designed to fool the algorithm, or machine drawing plans showing the needed end application. Some of them are illustrated in Fig. 1.

While different metrics have been proposed to evaluate the performance, the general consensus has been to use the one developed by Liu and Dori [17]. This metric will be detailed further in Sect. 4.1.

1.2   Reproducibilty

We are not going to reproduce an extensive overview of the many exiting algorithms for detecting circles, as will be explained further. The only way for evaluating performances of these multiple approaches consists of testing them on unified benchmarks. However, very often, when a circle detection algorithm is developed, the authors choose some images on which to test it. Often these images are small and simple and the algorithm performs well. When applied in real problems, however, the images for which the algorithm is needed, will not be small and simple. Often they will contain noise from aging while the document has been in storage, or from the acquisition process. These are specifically the cases for which circle detection is needed. Therefore the end user will care not about how the circle detection algorithm performs in the ideal case, but how it performs when under stress, or will like to use the algorithm best suited for their operational conditions (speed, precision, image noise ...).

The contests described in Sect. 1.1 provide an interesting step in the right direction, but fail to fully satisfy the actual goals. This is due to the following reasons:

1. They are time bound, and correspond to snapshots at the time they are run. Although the contests usually provide open access to their reference data sets, and therefore allow replay of the data on algorithms that were unavailable

at the time, this condition is not reversible, in a sense that the competing algorithms cannot be applied to other reference data.

2. Getting access to published algorithms that have competed in the past, is very often quite difficult.

3. Changing metrics is impossible.

4. When human annotated reference data is used, often multiple interpretations of ground truth are possible [13], and it is difficult to assess whether difference in precision performance of specific algorithms is due to the quality of the algorithms or quality of the reference data...

In this paper we introduce a method for comparing algorithms and to allow researchers to test their own work using shared and identical experimental conditions. Since the exact quality and quantity of noise is hard to measure on real scanned data, and the ground truth is hard to extract, we present a synthetic ground truth generator that is able to provide both realistic noise and drawing content. The code to create these images and to run the test procedure will be made available on the DAE platform [12].

2 Technical Background

Five different algorithms were used in this study. The choice of the actual algorithms was quite simple: we took those for which we were able to get a reliable implementation. This was either because their authors kindly provided us with their code or binaries, or because the algorithms were sufficiently documented in the supporting publications. A brief overview of each algorithm is presented here. Details for each algorithm are available in the referenced work. For a significant number of published methods, we failed to reach the authors or to correctly reimplement the algorithms based on the published descriptions only.

2.1 Hough 3D

The most well known and probably oldest method for finding a circle in an image the Hough Transform [9,21]. It is often also used as a baseline for performance comparison. It is based on having a circle

$$(x - x_c)^2 + (y - y_c)^2 = R^2 \tag{1}$$

with unknown parameters x_c, y_c and R. For every known "on" point (x, y) the set of the possible x_c, y_c and R that could produce a circle containing that point are listed. The algorithm creates an accumulator grid for x_c and y_c center coordinates and radius R that are candidate parameter values. Then for every point in the image that is "on", all the x_c, y_c and R that could correspond to it are incremented in the accumulator. The parameters corresponding to the accumulator bins where there is a peak are the parameters that correspond to circles in the image.

Implementing this requires a set of loops to map each "on" pixel to all the appropriate (x_c, y_c, R) accumulator bins. Finding the peaks heavily depends on the chosen bin resolution and on how many are selected from the accumulator. The number of peaks selected will determine the number of returned detected circles, but this needs also to be parametrized, either by setting an accumulator bin threshold level, or specifying the quantity of circles desired. It takes a fairly high amount of memory to store the accumulator array and also a fair amount of computational time to fill it. These operational requirements make it an undesirable algorithm to use in practice.

A number of well documented techniques for computational complexity reduction exist. Sometimes methods are used to reduce the number of "on" pixels that are used to fill the accumulator array, like those used in Sects. 2.2 and 2.3. As a comparison baseline, we have implemented a version of the Hough Transform that uses the basic algorithm with a 3-dimensional accumulator grid. To make the algorithm run in a reasonable amount of time and memory, we introduced some algorithmic accelerations, while making sure the final mapping to the 3D accumulator array from the original points continued as in the original algorithm.

In the 1000×1000 pixel images used in this project, on the order of 20,000 pixels were "on" pixels. For each pixel all eligible (x_c, y_c, R) must be incremented within the accumulator. To reduce this loop size, the image was reduced $5\times$ resulting in a $125\times$ smaller accumulator array. To not lose points because of sub sampling, the reduced image array was set to "on" if any of the pixels in the 5×5 window were "on" in the original image.

All (x_c, y_c, R) values that had an accumulation of 90% of the expected circumference at that radius size were identified. For all potential radius sizes identified in the prefiltering step, the (x_c, y_c, R) values were used as a mask to select (and reduce) "on" points in the original image. The points that satisfied the mask were processed with the full resolution 3D Hough Transform at each candidate radius. As per the Nixon implementation [21], the accumulator array was created and analyzed for each radius value separately in turn reducing memory requirements. The list of (x_c, y_c, R) values that had an accumulation of 90% of the expected circumference at this full resolution were stored. A 3D accumulator again at $5\times$ reduction was used to group these points using a connected component algorithm. The original high-resolution (x_c, y_c, R) values that correspond with each cluster were then used to identify the circle centers and radii. The average x_c, y_c and R values in each cluster were selected as algorithm outputs. The range of radii in each cluster was used to determine stroke width.

This algorithm was implemented in Matlab and takes between 2 and 4 min for each 1000 by 1000 image (without pepper noise) on both an older 32 bit laptop and on a server that for other algorithms provided greater than a $3\times$ speedup. When pepper noise is introduced, the run-time increases. At a pepper noise level of $P = 6$, it was taking 6 h per image. The results for $P \geq 6$ are therefore not shown.

2.2   Hough 2D - Hough Gradient Method

While the Hough 3D algorithm for circles is a standard, there are several variations to reduce its size and complexity. One algorithm related to Hough 3D and
often called Hough for circles is based on the idea that the gradient of the edges
of a circle will point toward the center of the circle. This algorithm is the one
used in the OpenCV package [22].

The algorithm starts by finding all Canny edges. This reduces the search
space from the original Hough algorithm. The gradient for each line in the image
is calculated. At each "on" pixel location, a line in drawn in the direction of
the gradient in a 2D accumulator space. Peaks in this accumulator space are
designated as circle centers. Then the L_2 distance from each point to each circle
center is calculated. If it is within the allowable radius range, an accumulator is
incremented.

2.3   Hough Gradients - Jia

This algorithm [10,11] is very similar to the Hough Gradient algorithm. The
source code for it written in Matlab was provided by its authors. The gradient
is used to find the intersection of lines and candidate circle centers. Then radii
are tried consecutively to see if within a small distance from the radius there are
many points with a high gradient. All radii that exceed a threshold are saved.
Then the list is parsed to eliminate radii that are consecutive.

The original algorithm was designed for use on small natural scene images.
We modified the source code provided by the authors to take advantage of Matlab vector processing accelerations. We also modified the algorithm that searches
for the circle's radius to indicate at which radii a large percentage of the circumference contains black pixels, instead of just a high gradient. This also reduced
the number of false concentric circles found.

2.4   QGAR Algorithm

This method was published in [14]. It being our own work, access to the source
code was straightforward. It is constructed around a robust estimator determining whether there is a circular arc close to a given center (x_c, y_c) and radius σ.
However, it needs some initial guess on where to search. It proceeds in three
main phases:

1. Generate a high number of possible arc candidates, without consideration of
   uniqueness, overlapping or exact localization. The arc candidates are obtained
   by operating a line extraction algorithm on the data, and by considering the
   circular arc defined by two connected line segments.
2. Verify the quality of each candidate using the approach described below. The
   output of this verification is a list of genuine arcs, correctly fitted on the
   image data.
3. Detect and merge multiple and/or partial detections of the same curves as to
   obtain a set of unique, disjoint arcs.

In order to evaluate the quality of an initial arc guess, the approach is to find a set $P = \{p_i\}$ of all image pixels p_i radially closest to the theoretical discrete circular arc $\mathcal{A}_0$ at iteration 0. P is then used for updating the estimate of the arc parameters, resulting in a new arc estimate $\mathcal{A}_1$ for which the process is iterated until convergence. At convergence a fitness measure, based on a threshold of image pixels lying on the arc determines whether the estimate is to be rejected or not.

2.5   ED Circles Algorithm

The ED Circles algorithm [2] is based on an edge segment detector (ED) algorithm [1] that joins sets of identified edge points into edge segments. This results in an edge map that is not a set of points, but a set of edge segments or pixel chains. Sets of consecutive line segments are evaluated to determine if they are candidates to be parts of lines, circles/arcs, or other. If the angle between the segments is less than 6° they are a considered colinear; if it is greater than 60°, then a corner is likely present, and the segments are separated. Consecutive line segments with an angle between 6 and 60° that turn in the same direction and have consistent angles values are defined as forming a circular arc.

Points corresponding to sets of segments that are candidates for a circle or arc are tested for a good least squares fit. If the fit is adequate, the next segment is a tried for addition of a following segment, otherwise the process stops and what is there is saved. Sets of arcs with calculated radii within constraints and close physical proximity are evaluated to see if they collectively form a circle.

As a final step the candidate lines, circles and arcs are validated with the Helmholz principle [8]. This looks at the probability that any mismatches (false alarms) occurred by chance.

Since EDCircles is designed to work on natural scene images, the edge detector will find both the interior and exterior edge on document images. We therefore modified the output such that, when two concentric circles (circles with center positions having an L_2 distance less than 10 pixels) were found with radii differing by less than 10 pixels, we averaged the center pixel coordinates and radii were averaged. The difference in the radii determines the stroke width.

The authors did not provide the source code for this algorithm, but they have a web portal [3] where images can be tested. They only output detected circles, even though their published algorithm is capable of detecting arcs and lines.

3   Data and Experimental Protocol

In order to provide a perfectly controlled, yet realistic experimental data set, we create images that contain a mixture of circles, arcs and straight lines with known positions and stroke thicknesses, as well as genuine noise. We want to create a large number of synthetic images with several noise levels and type.

Two types of noise were added to the images: edge noise and impulsive or pepper noise. While in physical documents both noise types can occur in the same image samples, the two types of noise are treated separately here to see the effect that each type of noise has on the circle and arc detection algorithms.

3.1 Edge Noise

The edge noise is based on image degradations produced by the Baird degradation model [6]. This models the bilevel image acquisition process, which contains blurring from the optics and additive Gaussian noise from the sensors. This is then thresholded with a global threshold to form a bilevel image. With a threshold at 50%, the position of the edge will not change, but corners (*e.g.* at intersections) will round slightly. In the gray-scale image before thresholding, the blurring smooths the transition of the amplitude from white to black. The additive noise on this sloped surface will at times be above the threshold and at times below the threshold. Therefore the noise will cause a variation in the pixels at the edge. The distance from the edge where the noise has this transition effect is called the Noise Spread (NS) [20]. We use 0.5, 1.0, 1.5 and 2.0 pixel NS (*cf.* Fig. 2). At larger values, the noise can exceed the threshold and cause isolated or impulsive noise. To separate the effects of the different noise types, all isolated pixels are filtered to white.

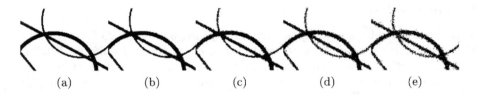

(a)   (b)   (c)   (d)   (e)

Fig. 2. Samples of images with varying levels of Noise Spread. (a) Original image without noise, (b) NS = 0.5, (c) NS = 1.0, (d) NS = 1.5, (e) NS = 2.0.

3.2 Impulsive Noise

The second type of noise is impulsive or pepper noise in which each pixel i is transformed into i_t with a probability

$$\mathbf{P}\left(i_t = black|_{i=white}\right) = \mathbf{P}_{pepper}$$
$$\mathbf{P}\left(i_t = white|_{i=black}\right) = \mathbf{P}_{salt}. \tag{2}$$

This is the noise that is more easy to see and is the type of noise used for the arc detection contest of GREC 2005. The physical source of this noise is the same as the source of the edge noise. It usually appears in systems where the sensor noise or the paper texture is great, and the binarization threshold is low. Edge noise will accompany it in physical systems. For this paper, the noise was added without blurring, as was the case in GREC 2005 and [19]. Therefore the edges have no transition zone between black and white (*i.e.* NS = 0). In this paper we use only pepper noise so the strokes are not affected directly.

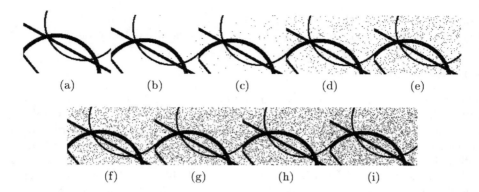

Fig. 3. Samples of images with varying levels of pepper noise. (a) Original image without noise, (b)–(i) $\mathbf{P}_{pepper} = 0.0005, 0.005, 0.026, 0.045, 0.073, 0.11, 0.125, 0.16$.

We empirically estimated $\mathbf{P}_{pepper}$ from the GREC 2005 dataset and determined eight levels: $\{0.0005, 0.005, 0.026, 0.045, 0.073, 0.11, 0.125, 0.16\}$. These are referenced as pepper noise levels $P = 1..8$ in the remainder of the paper (*cf.* Fig. 3).

3.3   Image Data

Images generated for this study all contain 5 circles, 5 arcs and 25 line segments. The circles have a random center and radius, drawn from a uniform distribution $U[100, 900]$ for the center coordinates, and $U[50, 200]$ for their radius. The arcs have a supplementary starting angle within $U[0, 360]$ and a span within $U[30, 180]$ degrees. The line segment end points were drawn from a random distribution $U[1, 1000]$. Each component has a randomly chosen stroke width between 2 and 7 pixels. To generate a line with a thickness, the object was created with a one pixel thickness and then morphologically dilated by a circle of the appropriate diameter.

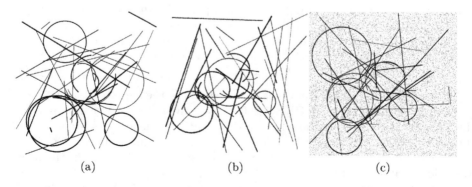

Fig. 4. Sample test images. (a) without noise (b) NS = 2.0 (c) Pepper = 0.045%.

We created 10 different randomly generated line drawings of size 1000×1000 (*cf.* Fig. 4). They were created initially at $4\times$ the resolution so the blurring process that creates the edge noise could be done with discrete convolution, and then downsampled to return the images to the "original" resolution. 10 instances of noise were added to each of the edge noise images at each noise level. 5 instances of noise were added to each of the impulse noise images. This produced a total of 100 noisy images for each noise level for edge noise and 50 for each impulse noise level. There were 400 total noisy images for each type of noise. There were 10 images without noise used as reference.

4   Experiments and Results

We compared the performance of five circle detection algorithms versus two types of noise at varying noise levels. We used two metrics to quantify their performance. We next discuss the metrics, and then show the performance of the algorithms.

4.1   Performance Metrics

Two performance metrics were used to evaluate the quality of the circle detection. The first is ArcEval by Liu and Dori [17], which is the one used in past GREC arc detection contests. It contains measurements of the amount of positive match between the estimated circles and the negative or false alarm mismatch between the two images. While the original paper includes multiple metrics we only consider the vector performance metrics, D_v, F_v, and VRI. The implementation we are using is the executable from the 2009 GREC contest.

The detection rate is

$$D_v = \frac{\sum_{g \in V_g} Q_v(g)l(g)}{\sum_{k \in V_d} l(g)}. \tag{3}$$

The quantity $Q_v(g)$ is the vector detection quantity and is made from a combination of the quality of the match in the endpoints, overlap distance, line width, line style and line shape. It can take values from 0 to 1, and a value of 1 is desired. V_g is the set of ground truth vec objects, and V_d is the set of detected vec objects. $l()$ is the length of the vec object stroke. The false alarm rate

$$F_v = \frac{\sum_{k \in V_d} F_v(k)l(k)}{\sum_{k \in V_d} l(k)} \tag{4}$$

is the length-weighted sum of the false alarm factors $F_v(k) = 1 - Q_v(k)$, meaning one minus the match of a line to the image that shouldn't have been there, or a 100% match to the background. We desire F_v to be zero. Similar to the F-measure in retrieval, the detection and false alarm rates are combined, but in a weighted arithmetic mean

$$VRI = \beta D_v + (1 - \beta)(1 - F_v). \tag{5}$$

The weight factor β is set to 0.5. We also want VRI to be 1.

The Liu–Dori metrics rely on the percent overlap of the detected strokes with the ground truth strokes. Some of the circle detection algorithms produce a list of circles that are plausible indicating the algorithm did indeed find real circles and not random noise, but have a one or two pixel error in the circle center position and/or the radius length. This can result in zero stroke overlap and thus a score of 0 for V_p, 1 for V_{fa} and 0 for VRI. This does not accurately reflect the algorithms' performance. Thus a second evaluation metric was created. This metric looks at the percent overlap of the circle area. To liken it to the Liu–Dori metric, a version for positive overlap, C_d, and false-alarm non-overlap, C_f, were created and then averaged. This starts with the overlap percentage calculated by

$$Ov(C_1, C_2) = \frac{\overline{C_1 \bigcap C_2}}{max(\overline{C_1}, \overline{C_2})}, \tag{6}$$

which is the area of the overlap between circle 1, C_1, and circle 2, C_2, divided by the maximum area of the circles individually. The overlap area is calculated algebraically [24] based on the vec data.

C_d measures for each ground truth circle, whether there is a detected circle that strongly overlaps ($\geq 50\%$) it and if so, their average overlap metric:

$$C_d = \sum_{g \in V_{gt}} Ov(C_{d^*}, C_{gt})/N_{gt}. \tag{7}$$

C_f measures the percentage of detected circles that do not have a match ($\geq 50\%$) with a ground truth circle

$$C_f = 1 - \sum_{d \in V_d} Ov(C_d, C_{gt})/N_d. \tag{8}$$

For each circle this requires finding which ground truth circle is the best match to it, so it will only be used once in the match calculations. For instance, we do not want several circle overlapping one ground truth circle to all count as positive matches. The excess ones are false alarms and should penalize the algorithm. As in Eq. 5 the detection and false alarm rates are averaged

$$VRI_C = \beta D_v + (1 - \beta)(1 - F_v). \tag{9}$$

This metric is currently implemented only for circles. Detected arcs are ignored, and lack of properly detected arcs is not penalized.

4.2 Results

The 10 original and 800 noisy images were processed by each of the five circle detection algorithms. The match between the estimated results and the ground truth was calculated with the two methods described in Sect. 4.1. For each noise level and image combination the average across the noise instances was calculated.

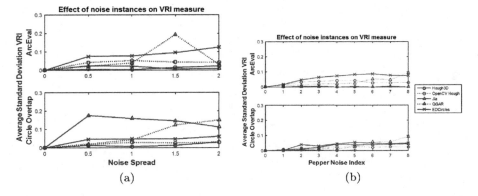

Fig. 5. The standard deviation of VRI across the (a) 10 edge spread instances and (b) 5 pepper noise instance averaged over 10 images.

Multiple noise instances were used for each image and noise level (10 instances for edge noise and 5 instances for pepper noise) to reduce the chance of specific noise pixels significantly affecting the results. Figure 5 shows the standard deviation measured across the noise instances and then averaged across the 10 different images. The standard deviation of the performance measurements was very low between noise instances. The different noise instances have a smaller effect for the pepper noise.

Edge noise results: The average VRI for both metrics across the 10 instances and 10 images for each algorithm was calculated for each noise level. The results are shown in Fig. 6. As expected, the performance of the algorithms decreased as the amount of noise was increased, but for most algorithms not in as extreme

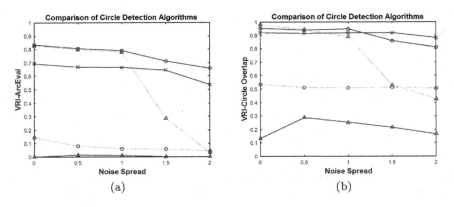

Fig. 6. The average VRI across the 10 instances and 10 images for edge noise (a) Liu–Dori metric (b) Circle overlap metric. The legend is as in Fig. 5.

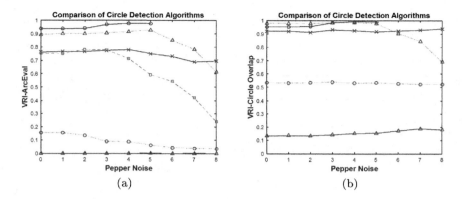

Fig. 7. The average VRI across the 5 instances and 10 images for pepper noise (a) Liu–Dori metric (b) Circle overlap metric. The legend is as in Fig. 5. In Figure (a) the dashed line with square symbols is results from paper [19]

a fashion as expected. The Hough 3D algorithm was overall the best performer even though it did not detect arcs. The Qgar circle detection algorithm had the highest performance scores at low noise levels. The EDCircles algorithm was least sensitive to the noise, maintaining a VRI score of 0.7 for the ArcEval metric and a VRI score of 0.9 with the circle overlap method. The OpenCV Hough and the Jia algorithm scored very low with the Liu–Dori metrics because of small radius estimate errors resulting in strokes not physically overlapping. While they did not perform strongly with the circle overlap metric, it can be seen that they do detect some circles with reasonable accuracy.

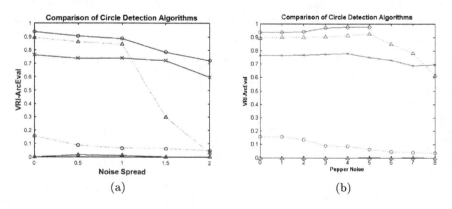

Fig. 8. The average Liu–Dori VRI across the 10 images for (a) edge and (b) pepper noise when arcs are eliminated from the ground truth. The legend is as in Fig. 5.

Pepper noise results: The average VRI across the 5 pepper noise instances and 10 images is shown in Fig. 7. A similar trend is seen relative to increased pepper noise level as was seen for edge noise. Hough 3D is the strongest and Qgar is most affected by noise. The algorithms were not affected as much by the pepper noise as they were by the edge noise.

Figure 7(a) also includes the results for the Liu–Dori VRI metric from their paper [19]. It has the same pepper noise levels, but also includes salt noise and is on different image content. It gives some level of comparison as their algorithm is not available to test here.

Full circles only: The OpenCV Hough and the Jia method were only designed to detect full circles. While EDCircles is capable of detecting arcs, their online service only returns circles and ellipses. Therefore to evaluate their performance, all the arcs were removed from the ground truth vec files for consideration by the Liu-Dori evaluation metric. Those results are shown in Fig. 8. The results have the same shape with and without the arcs. The arcs would have added a false alarm quantity to all images the same across all noise levels appearing as a bias. Their removal reduced that in those algorithms.

Samples of detection results: In Fig. 9 the arcs and circles identified by two of the algorithms can be seen. The Qgar algorithm is the only one that detects arcs. The Jia algorithm sometimes detects arcs as circles, but has many false alarms. Thus the difference in the VRI scores for the Liu–Dori metric versus the circle overlap metrics can be better understood.

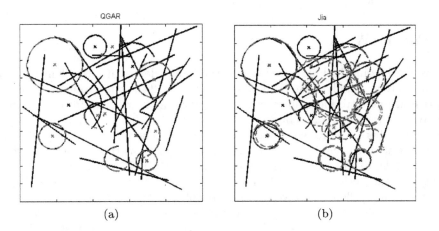

(a)   (b)

Fig. 9. The original image and the detected results for (a) Qgar and (b) Jia. Image 8, NS = 0.5, noise instance 2.

5   Conclusion

We have expanded the existing generally admitted framework for evaluating the robustness of circle and arc detection algorithms to different types of noise and have introduced a complementary performance metric based on circle overlap.

The main contribution of this paper is that it provides a finer way to compare algorithms, or to evaluate an individual individually to assess its suitability under well defined operational conditions, without the cost of manually annotating scanned documents.

We have provided two data sets, one for edge noise and one for pepper noise, and the source code for generating new sets is equally publicly available.

From our experiments on various state-of-the-art circle detection algorithms we can conclude that:

– Our noise model produces very consistent performance behaviours over all evaluated models.
– Our new evaluation metric, based on circle overlap surfaces, provides performance readings that are consistent with the usual Liu-Dori metrics. However, results are not identical, and underscore that the choice of metrics is important in regard to the application context.
– Reproducibility and traceability of published results remains a difficult issue. Not all contacted authors were willing or capable of providing source code or binaries of their published work. Sometimes provided code was not consistent with the claimed results, or needed debugging. Reprogramming from the published algorithm description was also, in one case, challenging.
  As a result, there are only 2 cases where we are certain to test against the actual, previously published algorithms.

6   Future Work

Future work could include variations in the image deformations. Elongation of the circles to gradually make them more elliptical will show the robustness of the algorithm, but introduces an interpretative bias, as it will require us to define the "best" circle fitting an ellipse.

The number of extraneous lines can be varied. There are currently 25 lines interfering with the circles and arcs. For some algorithms this is not a problem. For other algorithms, intersecting lines significantly reduce performance. Analyzing how the performance is degraded by extraneous lines is interesting, as is the detection of filled circles versus the current non-filled circles.

Furthermore, in some of our experiments we have observed unexpected behaviour of the Liu–Dori metric. We will investigate this matter further to determine whether this is an inherent shortcoming of the method, or has some other cause.

Integrating the image generation and the performance evaluation software into the DAE [12] platform will allow all researchers to evaluate their algorithms under this framework and will allow them to duplicate the results in this paper relative to those algorithms.

Acknowledgment. The authors would like to thank *Télécom Nancy* students G. Humbert and Y. Jardin for their preliminary work, and all authors who were solicited and who kindly provided their source code, binary code or other contribution allowing us to fully evaluate their methods. E. Barney Smith was funded under the *"Chercheur d'excellence"* program by the *Région Lorraine*.

References

1. Akinlar, C., Topal, C.: EDLines: a real-time line segment detector with a false detection control. Pattern Recognit. Lett. **32**(13), 1633–1642 (2011)
2. Akinlar, C., Topal, C.: EDCircles: a real-time circle detector with a false detection control. Pattern Recognit. **46**, 725–740 (2013)
3. Akinlar, C., Topal, C.: EDCircles Web Interface (2015). http://ceng.anadolu.edu.tr/CV/EDCircles/demo.aspx. Accessed 6 May 2015
4. Al-Khaffaf, H.S.M., Talib, A.Z., Osman, M.A., Wong, P.L.: GREC'09 arc segmentation contest: performance evaluation on old documents. In: Ogier, J.-M., Liu, W., Lladós, J. (eds.) GREC 2009. LNCS, vol. 6020, pp. 251–259. Springer, Heidelberg (2010). doi:10.1007/978-3-642-13728-0_23
5. Al-Khaffaf, H.S.M., Talib, A.Z., Osman, M.A.: Final report of GREC'11 arc segmentation contest: performance evaluation on multi-resolution scanned documents. In: Kwon, Y.-B., Ogier, J.-M. (eds.) GREC 2011. LNCS, vol. 7423, pp. 187–197. Springer, Heidelberg (2013). doi:10.1007/978-3-642-36824-0_18
6. Baird, H.S.: Document image defect models. In: Proceedings of the IAPR Workshop on Syntactic and Structural Pattern Recognition, pp. 13–15. Murray Hill, NJ, June 1990. Reprinted: Baird, H.S., Bunke, H., Yamamoto, K. (eds.) Structured Document Image Analysis. Springer, New York (1992)
7. Bukhari, S.S., Al-Khaffaf, H.S.M., Shafait, F., Osman, M.A., Talib, A.Z., Breuel, T.M.: Final report of GREC'13 arc and line segmentation contest. In: Lamiroy, B., Ogier, J.-M. (eds.) GREC 2013. LNCS, vol. 8746, pp. 234–239. Springer, Heidelberg (2014). doi:10.1007/978-3-662-44854-0_18
8. Desolneux, A., Moisan, L., Morel, J.: From Gestalt Theory to Image Analysis: A Probabilisitc Approach. Springer, New York (2008)
9. Hough, P.: Methods and means for recognizing complex patterns (1962)
10. Jia, L.Q., Peng, C.Z.: A new circle detection method based on parallel operator. In: 2012 International Conference on Machine Learning and Cybernetics (ICMLC), vol. 3, pp. 1085–1090 (2012)
11. Jia, L.Q., Peng, C.Z., Liu, H.M., Wang, Z.H.: A fast randomized circle detection algorithm. In: 2011 4th International Congress on Image and Signal Processing (CISP), vol. 2, pp. 820–823 (2011)
12. Lamiroy, B., Lopresti, D.: An open architecture for end-to-end document analysis benchmarking. In: 2011 International Conference on Document Analysis and Recognition (ICDAR), pp. 42–47, September 2011
13. Lamiroy, B.: Interpretation, evaluation and the semantic gap.. What if we were on a side-track? In: Lamiroy, B., Ogier, J.-M. (eds.) GREC 2013. LNCS, vol. 8746, pp. 221–233. Springer, Heidelberg (2014). doi:10.1007/978-3-662-44854-0_17

14. Lamiroy, B., Guebbas, Y.: Robust and precise circular arc detection. In: Ogier, J.-M., Liu, W., Lladós, J. (eds.) GREC 2009. LNCS, vol. 6020, pp. 49–60. Springer, Heidelberg (2010). doi:10.1007/978-3-642-13728-0_5

15. Liu, W.: Report of the arc segmentation contest. In: Lladós, J., Kwon, Y.-B. (eds.) GREC 2003. LNCS, vol. 3088, pp. 364–367. Springer, Heidelberg (2004). doi:10.1007/978-3-540-25977-0_33

16. Wenyin, L.: The third report of the arc segmentation contest. In: Liu, W., Lladós, J. (eds.) GREC 2005. LNCS, vol. 3926, pp. 358–361. Springer, Heidelberg (2006). doi:10.1007/11767978_32

17. Liu, W., Dori, D.: A protocol for performance evaluation of line detection algorithms. Mach. Vis. Appl. **9**, 240–250 (1997)

18. Liu, W., Zhai, J., Dori, D.: Extended summary of the arc segmentation contest. In: Blostein, D., Kwon, Y.-B. (eds.) GREC 2001. LNCS, vol. 2390, pp. 343–349. Springer, Heidelberg (2002). doi:10.1007/3-540-45868-9_30

19. Liu, W., Zhai, J., Dori, D., Long, T.: System for performance evaluation of arc segmentation algorithms. In: Proceedings of the CVPR Workshop Empirical Evaluation in Computer Vision (2001)

20. McGillivary, C., Hale, C., Smith, E.H.B.: Edge noise in document images. In: Proceedings of the 3rd Workshop on Analytics for Noisy Unstructured Text Data, pp. 17–24 (2009)

21. Nixon, M., Aguado, A.: Feature Extraction & Image Processing, 2nd edn. Academic Press, Oxford (2008)

22. OpenCV: Hough Circle Transform (2015). http://docs.opencv.org/doc/tutorials/imgproc/imgtrans/hough_circle/hough_circle.html. Accessed 13 May 2015

23. Shafait, F., Keysers, D., Breuel, T.M.: GREC 2007 arc segmentation contest: evaluation of four participating algorithms. In: Liu, W., Lladós, J., Ogier, J.-M. (eds.) GREC 2007. LNCS, vol. 5046, pp. 310–320. Springer, Heidelberg (2008). doi:10.1007/978-3-540-88188-9_29

24. Wolfram MathWorld: Circle-Circle Intersection (2015). http://mathworld.wolfram.com/Circle-CircleIntersection.html. Accessed 13 May 2015

The Creation of Synthetic Digital Ground-Truth Images of Historic Cosmic Ray Data Recordings

Vincent Mattana, Günther Drevin$^{(\boxtimes)}$, and Pierre Roux

North-West University, Potchefstroom Campus, Potchefstroom, South Africa
gunther.drevin@nwu.ac.za

Abstract. The aim of this paper is to develop a set of algorithms for the automated construction of synthetic digital ground truth images from historic cosmic ray recordings. These images can subsequently be used to test data extraction algorithms. This takes place in a larger research context of an effort to retrieve and digitize the data contained within more than 20 years (1934–1956) of historic cosmic ray data from around the world. The creation of synthetic ground truth images can logically be broken down into component tasks, which can be approached individually. These tasks include: binarization, segmentation, as well as generation of optical artefacts and distortions. The approach and details of the algorithm are described.

Keywords: Image processing · Cosmic rays · Segmentation · Digitization · Degrade · Document images · Local adaptive binarization · Soft decisions

1 Introduction

The aim of this project is to develop a set of algorithms to automatically construct synthetic ground-truth images from historic cosmic ray recordings which can be used to compare the accuracy and efficiency of different interpretation and data extraction algorithms. When designing a data extraction algorithm, ground truth images are required to score the algorithm's performance and to compare it to other algorithms. These synthetic ground truth images are critical in rating the accuracy of the algorithms. In a sense this is the first step towards the complete extraction and interpretation of historic cosmic ray recordings. The future steps could include data detection, extraction of the numeric values represented by these data recordings, as well as interpretation of these results (which document the ionization levels in a cosmic ray detector). Eventually the cosmic ray data contained within these recordings could be released for further study. However, that is beyond the scope of this project, in which the goal is to create a synthetic ground truth image, which replicates the condition and appearance of the recorded data, as well as having a benchmark against which to test competing algorithms in the following steps of the data rescue effort. The synthetic image must however contain some degree of distortion, so that

© Springer International Publishing AG 2017
B. Lamiroy and R. Dueire Lins (Eds.): GREC 2015, LNCS 9657, pp. 19–30, 2017.
DOI: 10.1007/978-3-319-52159-6_2

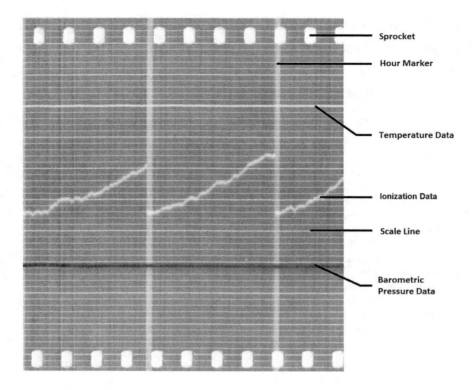

Sprocket

Hour Marker

Temperature Data

Ionization Data

Scale Line

Barometric
Pressure Data

Fig. 1. Diagram of an original section of the photographic paper.

the tested algorithm can function in an environment as similar to the original image as possible [3]. This is because the more similar the synthetic image is to the original, the more relevant the results of the testing of the algorithms will be. Once the ground truth and synthetic images are complete and verified, the algorithms responsible for their creation can potentially be integrated into the data extraction and interpretation algorithms, to provide accuracy statistics on the results.

1.1   The Model C Detector

The Carnegie Institute funded a project to develop a precision cosmic ray recorder, which was undertaken by Compton *et al.* [1]. A number of these devices, the Model C cosmic ray ionization chamber (henceforth the Model C detector), were manufactured by the team [1]. Each of them recorded cosmic ray data on photographic paper.

The true value of these recordings lies in the massive collection of data that was generated from the manufacture of the recording devices, in 1934, up to 1956 when neutron monitors began to replace the Model C detectors.

More than a 100 station-years of recordings were generated by the Model C detector. The structure of the images on these photographic papers can be described by investigating their components as well as the recording process: Each image consists of horizontal scale lines and vertical hour and day markers, Fig. 1. Additionally, there are data recordings for cosmic ray intensity, barometric pressure, and temperature. The cosmic ray intensity was recorded continuously by recording the electric charge accumulating in the ionization chamber, Fig. 2. The recording process involves the mounting of the recording paper onto a sprocket drive, aligning the scale grid, as well the recording needles. It is assumed that adjustments were not performed perfectly every time due to human error, and as such could have led to distortions within the recordings, which will be discussed later. The contrast and quality of the images also vary due to inconsistencies in the chemical processing of the photographic paper.

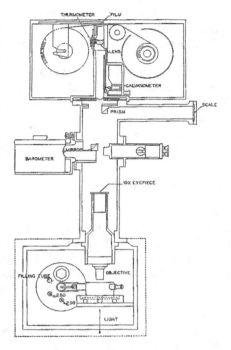

Fig. 2. Detailed drawing of electrometer box, optical system, barometer, and recording camera. Adapted from [1].

Other examples of distortions include hand written annotations, punched holes, and stickers. Furthermore bleed-through of annotations on the back of the photographic paper are also present.

2   Methodology

The method used for this study can be described as the hypothetico-deductive method [2]. Our approach followed a step-wise improvement of the source image, and is described by the following steps:

1. Increasing the contrast of an original image.
2. Binarization of the resulting image.
3. Segmentation of the image to extract components of the image such as hour markers, scale lines, data lines and sprockets.
4. Production of an approximate ground truth image, using the segmented image.
5. Mapping of distortions and optical artefacts found in the original images onto the ground truth image, to produce a synthetic image.

6. Creation of a textured synthetic image, using a texture only image created from an original image.
7. Comparison of the synthetic image to the original image.

The photographic paper that the image is recorded on can contribute to the graininess of the image, and any imperfections of the material used to record the original document will be carried over into the digital format. The process of scanning these photographic papers was undertaken by a private contractor. The images measure approximately 6000 by 905 pixels, have a pixel depth of 24 bits, and on average document a 19 h period.

2.1   Contrast Correction

The first step in creating ground truth data is to perform contrast correction on the source image. The generation of a ground truth data image is simplified by using a single high quality source image such as Christchurch 1937-08-02 Fig. 3. This image was selected due to its good condition, and each element of the recording was immediately recognizable by inspection. Global histogram equalization was used to improve the contrast of this image.

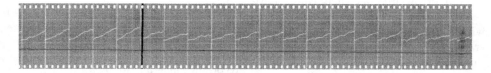

Fig. 3. The single high quality source image used (Christchurch 1937-08-02).

2.2   Binarization

The process of preparing a document image for the extraction of text from the document is known as document image binarization, however the intermediate steps of this method has much potential for segmenting the cosmic ray recordings. Many different techniques for document image binarization have been proposed, and could be used to binarize the historic cosmic ray recordings, but the work of Sauvola and Pietikainen [11] and the improvements made thereupon by Gatos *et al.* [5] were the most effective in our application (Fig. 4). Otsu's method [8] was also used to isolate the hour markers. These techniques have all the necessary methods we need for the binarization of the historic cosmic ray recordings. Another option is adaptive thresholding, which selects different threshold values for different regions, by inspecting the gray-level intensities in a mask across the image. A number of different adaptive thresholding algorithms exist, such as Niblack's algorithm [6], which is built upon by Sauvola and Pietikainen [11], and then further refined by Gatos *et al.* [5], by using an adaptive Weiner filter to remove noise.

A difficulty in adaptive binarization is that a decision has to be made on the size of the mask to be used. The mask must be big enough to ensure that a sufficient selection of background (texture) pixels are captured, while maintaining a small enough footprint as to prevent the averaging of background pixels over nonuniform intensities. To counteract this, domain based information is used to check that the results give expected values [7]. It is essential to remove any noise or artefacts in an image before binarization since this can become detrimental in the later steps. If the image contains any texture, it is important to do contrast enhancement so that the foreground elements become more apparent from the background. This is achieved by using an adaptive Weiner filter, which uses statistics from local neighbouring pixels.

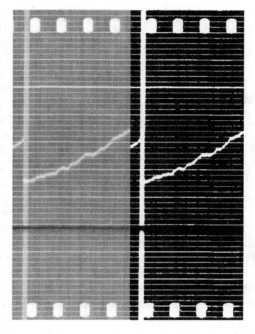

Fig. 4. The result of binarizing the image on the left.

2.3   Segmentation

Document image processing is concerned with all aspects of "working with" documents, from scanning through all the pre-processing steps to the final information extraction and recognition. Many algorithms exist within this field to extract text from documents, using segmentation, which can be described as the division of the image into logically distinct segments. These algorithms can be adapted to fit the needs of our objective, namely the creation of a ground truth image, which will eventually be distorted from its ideal condition to produce a synthetic image, which is comparable to the original image. The segmentation of the image is an iterative process, eliminating certain elements in an effort to isolate a specific attribute. Once an attribute of the ground truth image has been extracted, the algorithm reverts to working from an earlier version of the image, usually the binarized image. The image is then processed again to yield only the desired attribute. A number of different techniques were used, depending on the properties of the attribute to be extracted. The attributes that were extracted are shown in Fig. 1, and will be discussed now.

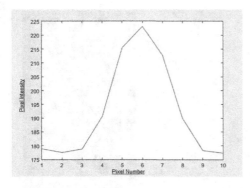

Fig. 5. Cross section of a scale line.

The Scale Lines. Scale lines run horizontally along the photographic paper, varying slightly over the length of the recording. Exploiting this directionality simply requires using a horizontal Prewitt filter [10] to only detect horizontal edges. The scale lines are represented by double edges on the resulting image. These double edges are filled by using morphological filtering in the vertical direction. The result is a line a few pixels thicker than the original. The scale lines however are still disrupted by the edges of intervening data lines. This effect is removed by using horizontal morphological filtering. The result is an image of thinner scale lines, disrupted only by the position of sprockets, temperature data, cosmic ray data, barometric pressure data and hour lines. To proceed further one must determine the number of the scale lines, as well as their positions. The height of the image, divided by the number of scale lines results in the number of pixels that should ideally be between successive scale lines. This information, along with the positions, are used to generate an ideal image of approximated scale lines. With the use of an ideal scale line image, it becomes a simple task to obtain samples of data for each individual scale line by following a line on the ideal model of the scale lines, with a seek range of up to half the number of pixels between each scale line. These samples are in turn used in regression analysis to determine a best fit linear function for the given data. The regression of the scale lines is based on the original image, and as such the ground truth scale lines are accurate representations thereof. A cross section of a typical scale line is shown in Fig. 5.

The Hour Markers. The same approach used to extract the scale lines will not work on the hour markers. Even if the Prewitt filters [10] are rotated 90°, there will still be false hour markers generated, since the majority of historic cosmic ray recordings contain spurious vertical edges. This is mainly attributed to the motion of the photographic paper moving through the recording device, which is not precisely constant nor uniform. A different approach was taken: By using the disruptions in the scale lines (in the binarized image of scale lines) the hour marker positions are clearly visible as gaps in the scale lines. This process is automated by using a parameter defining a threshold for locating the hour markers from gaps in the scale lines. Once these position are identified, ideal vertical lines are inserted at these locations. The hour markers are approximated using the average-pixels-between method and are then thinned to produce the ground truth hour markers. This effect is dependent on scale lines being appropriately located. Bearing in mind that the recording images each document a period of 19 h, a neighbourhood around the detected hour markers was inspected for any other detected hour markings, which could be false positives, as hour markers should appear approximately every 285 pixels, as an hour is approximately 300 pixels. Each hour marker has a width of approximately 15 pixels which represents 3 min of recording time, during which the ionization chamber was grounded.

The Sprockets. The tiny holes at the top and bottom edge of the photographic paper, are referred to as sprockets, and are used to advance the photographic paper. These sprockets are shaped like a flattened circle. The sprockets are located in a binarized, and smoothed image, where only the faintest remains of the sprockets are present. From this image it is

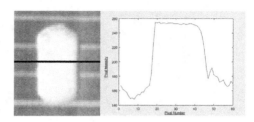

Fig. 6. A sample sprocket image and cross section of a typical sprocket hole.

possible to locate the sprocket "seed" positions, and construct an ideal sprocket at the location of each "seed" pixel. To simulate the shading found in the original image, a copy of the ideal sprocket image was used, and buffered (shifted 3 pixels towards the centre). This buffered image was then subtracted from the original, and a motion blur filter was applied to roughen the edges. A sample sprocket image and cross section of a typical sprocket hole is shown in Fig. 6.

Data Lines. There are 3 types of data recorded on the image. The thinner horizontal line represents the temperature data, the discontinuous line represents the cosmic ray ionization values, and the thicker, dark, horizontal line represents

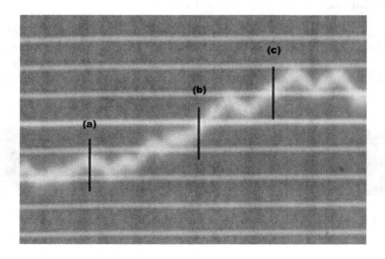

Fig. 7. Cosmic ray data line cross sections taken along the lines.

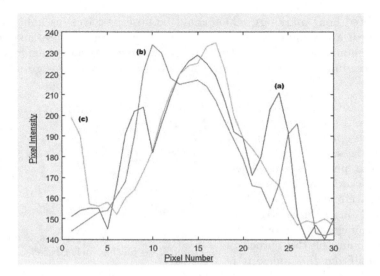

Fig. 8. Cross section of the cosmic ray data line, taken at varying points.

the barometric pressure. Ideally, the data lines would be extracted automatically, however, doing so reliably is difficult on some images. The data was instead extracted using a cursor to select data lines. This lets one determine the centre of the line, giving an indication of where the data lines can be found on the original image. This forms the basis for the data lines in the ground truth image. Cross sections of the data line at varying points are shown in Figs. 7 and 8.

2.4   Production of Ground-Truth Images

The final ground truth image is produced by adding together all the attribute images obtained while performing segmentation. This ground truth image represents the core elements of the original image. As this is a ground truth image, there is no texture, nor distortions included. The texture, and distortions will be discussed in the next section. The result is shown in Fig. 9.

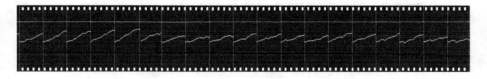

Fig. 9. The result of combining the composite segmented images.

2.5   Distortions

At this stage, the ground truth image has been produced with single pixel thick scale lines and data lines, as well as accurate hour markers, and sprockets. However, one will notice that this ground truth image does not resemble the original image, other than as a representation of the data elements contained in the original image. Thus the ground truth image has to be modified by some degree to represent the source image's texture and distortions. This is accomplished in a modular fashion, repeating similar algorithms for each component of the image.

Two main features of distortion are prominent in the hour markers, namely: edge sharpness and rotation [4]. Hour markers are produced on the photographic paper by deactivating the lamp for three minutes every hour. The orientation of the slit, however, is not always perfectly vertical. The angular rotation of the hour markers is found using the angle between the regressed scale lines and the ideal hour markers. These hour markers overlap with scale lines, and as such, the scale line intensities are subtracted before any smoothing is applied. The scale lines were distorted using a Gaussian filter that simulates the interference pattern of light, when passed through a narrow slit.

The majority of each sprocket is undistorted. However, one can see shadows cast by the photographic paper when comparing ideal sprockets to the sprockets on the original image (these distortions are mainly due to a lack of light and is perceived as a shadow of the image). Such shadows are added to ideal sprockets by adding a gradient filter over the ideal sprocket. It can be noted that the sprockets are the largest of the artefacts, as they affect the photographic film itself. This allows us to assume that there is no useful information to be gained in the sprocket areas, and as such can be disregarded in future algorithmic steps.

The data lines on the photographic paper are blurred, and do not have sharp edges. The distortion algorithm mimics this imprecision with a collection of image processing techniques tailored to simulating the histogram of the corresponding data line. This process results in a distorted ideal data line nearly identical to the source image's data line.

Reproducing Optical Artefacts. When considering the effects that occur regarding light and photographic paper, it is important to remember two things. The first thing to remember is that the real world is continuous, and not discrete like the digital world. The second thing to bear in mind is that when two waves superimpose, the resultant wave has either greater or smaller amplitude than the source waves. This physical phenomenon is referred to as interference, and it can cause ringing, an effect which causes dilation of point like illumination with bands of bright and dark. Usually these bands are so close to each other, and also moving, that they are blurred on the photographic paper. This blurring and ringing results in a broader and less defined data line. Thus it is necessary to generate such a distortion for the synthetic image. Various methods exist to achieve the desired results, and the fastest computational method was selected: By subtracting a slightly blurred image from a heavily blurred image, the results show a thin "ringing" around the original object. When this image and the distortions of all the attributes are added together, the resulting image contains optical artefacts, resembling the original distortions closely.

2.6   Texture

The texturing process is accomplished through a number of steps. The first step is to replace all the attributes' pixels with pixels from nearby texture regions. This image is then smoothed, and a histogram equalized version of the image is subtracted from this smoothed image, resulting in a mid-tone texture only image. From this point, the mid-tone image is binarized, once with a low threshold, and again with a high threshold. These binarized images represent the highlights, and darker regions of the image, respectively. Both of these binarized images are then added to the mid-tone image to yield the texture only image. This texture-only image is then combined with the distorted ground truth image to produce the result seen in Fig. 10.

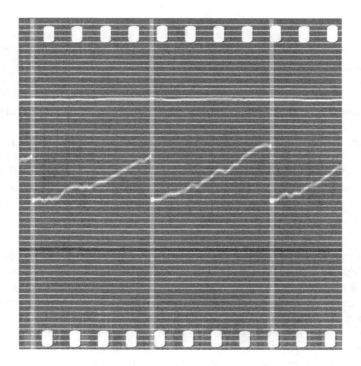

Fig. 10. The result of adding the texture to the distorted ground truth image, yielding the synthetic image.

3   Results

To adequately find a measure of success, the accuracy of the ground truth attributes was determined. The algorithm was tested by creating synthetic images from images of differing quality: Good, average and poor. These are each a single recording from: Christchurch (1937-08-02), Fredericksburg (1958-08-02) and Christchurch (1945-11-03), respectively. These historic recordings all have a similar recording format in common, in that all attributes have the same colour/intensity relative to their background. This is important to note, as some images have black hour markers, or other discrepancies. Comparison of image transformation algorithms can be done empirically by measuring the Mean Square Error (MSE) of each image [9]. However this will not suffice for the task at hand, since the synthetic generation of a texture will differ greatly in pixel intensities at specific coordinates which will in turn influence the MSE. The texture might be visually very similar to that of the source image, but the same result will not be represented by its MSE. Because of this, the texture and colour/intensity distortions are very subjective attributes to compare. Attributes such as scale lines, hour markers and sprockets will have their measure of success determined by the number of attributes matching the source image. To compare the results more clearly, the synthesised image was overlaid on the original image. These attributes are then coloured, and the attributes where compared. The results of this comparison are shown in Table 1.

Table 1. Empirical analysis of results

Measure	CHE ('37-08-02)	FRE ('58-08-02)	CHE ('45-11-03)	Average Accuracy
Scale lines	54/56	53/56	51/56	94.05 %
Hour markers	20/20	13/20	8/20	68.33 %
Sprockets	140/144	142/144	32/144	72.69 %
Texture	8/10	7/10	4/10	63.33 %
Data line consistency	19/20	13/20	15/20	78.33 %
Accuracy	93.73 %	78.65 %	53.66 %	75.35 %

4   Conclusion and Further Work

The aim of this study was to create a digital synthetic ground truth image from existing historic cosmic ray records. The goal of creating an image similar to the source image, while also containing the ground truth data, has been sufficiently achieved. The algorithms perform adequately under ideal circumstances, however, it preforms less effectively when applied to low quality source images. Improvements can be made to the texturing process, the automated thresholding for binarization, the data line and hour marker extraction, as well as compensating for the inherent angling (or tilt) in some of the hour markers and scale lines.

References

1. Compton, A.H., Wollan, E.O., Bennett, R.D.: A precision recording cosmic-ray meter. Rev. Sci. Instrum. **5**, 415–422 (1934)
2. Dodig-Crnkovic, G.: Scientific methods in computer science. In: Proceedings of the Conference for the Promotion of Research in IT at New Universities and at University Colleges in Sweden, Skövde, Suecia, pp. 126–130 (2002)
3. Drevin, G.R.: Adaptive frequency domain filtering of legacy cosmic ray recordings. In: Proceedings of the 11th Joint Conference on Information Sciences, pp. 15–20 (2008)
4. Drevin, G.R., Moraal, H., McCracken, K.G.: Determining the skew and scale in images of Compton-Wollan-Bennett ionization chamber recordings. Information Sciences 2007, pp. 888–894. World Scientific, Singapore (2007)
5. Gatos, B., Praktikakis, I., Perantonis, S.J.: Adaptive degraded document image binarization. Pattern Recogn. **39**, 317–327 (2006)
6. Niblack, W.: An Introduction to Digital Image Processing. Prentice-Hall, Upper Saddle River (1985)
7. O'Gorman, L., Katsuri, R.: Document Image Analysis. IEEE, New York (1997)
8. Otsu, N.: A thresholding selection method from gray-level histograms. Automatica **11**(285–296), 23–27 (1975)
9. Ponomarenko, N., Krivenko, S., Egiazarian, K., Astola, J., Lukin, V.: Weighted MSE based metrics for characterization of visual quality of image denoising methods. In: Proceedings of the 8th International Workshop on Video Processing and Quality Metrics for Consumer Electronics (VPQM 2014) (2014)
10. Prewitt, J.M.S.: Object enhancement and extraction. Picture Process. Psychopictorics **10**(1), 15–19 (1970)
11. Sauvola, J., Pietikäinen, M.: Adaptive document image binarization. Pattern Recogn. **33**, 225–236 (2000)

Statistical Performance Metrics for Use with Imprecise Ground-Truth

Bart Lamiroy[1(✉)] and Pascal Pierrot[2]

[1] Université de Lorraine, Loria (UMR 7503) Campus Scientifique – BP 239,
54506 Vandœuvre-lès-Nancy cedex, France
bart.lamiroy@loria.fr

[2] Université de Lorraine, Mines Nancy Campus Artem - CS 14 234, 92 Rue Sergent
Blandan, 54042 Nancy, France

Abstract. This paper addresses performance evaluation in the presence of imprecise ground-truth. Indeed, the most common assumption when performing benchmarking measures is that the reference data is flawless. In previous work, we have shown that this assumption cannot be taken for granted, and that, in the case of perceptual interpretation problems it is most certainly always wrong but for the most trivial cases.

We are presenting a statistical test that will allow measuring the confidence one can have in the results of a benchmarking test ranking multiple algorithms. More specifically, we can express the probability of the ranking not being respected in the presence of a given level of errors in the ground truth data.

1 Introduction

In this paper we investigate statistical tests for assessing the risk of misranking algorithms on benchmarks when using unreliable ground truth. The current approach to performance analysis is that algorithms assumed to be tested on totally reliable ground truth. We have shown in previous work that this assumption is flawed, and that there is an inherent interpretative bias in the definition of ground truth.

This paper is a first tentative step in creating a mathematically sound framework for assessing the risk of relying on imprecise ground truth. Indeed, the probability of algorithms being misranked is directly dependent on their overall performance on the one hand, and the level of error in the used ground truth.

This framework can be applied to benchmarking and contests (*e.g.* the GREC Arc Detection contests [1–3,7] or more general benchmarking environments [6])

2 Problem Description

2.1 Definitions and Notations

In this section we introduce all definitions and notations we use throughout this paper.

© Springer International Publishing AG 2017
B. Lamiroy and R. Dueire Lins (Eds.): GREC 2015, LNCS 9657, pp. 31–44, 2017.
DOI: 10.1007/978-3-319-52159-6_3

Let $\Phi = \{\phi_1, ..., \phi_p\}$ be a set of data, $\mathcal{I} = \{i_1, ..., i_q\}$ a finite set of possible interpretations over Φ and $\mathsf{A} = \{A_1, ..., A_n\}$ a set of algorithms.

First, we define the notion of *Ground Truth*, which associates a truth value to the interpretation i of a given data element d.

Definition 1 (Ground Truth). *A ground truth is a function Ω such that:*

$$\Omega : \Phi \times \mathcal{I} \to \{0, 1\}$$
$$(\phi, i) \mapsto \begin{cases} 1 \text{ iff } i \text{ is a correct interpretation for } \phi \\ 0 \text{ otherwise} \end{cases}$$

Definition 2 (Algorithm). *An algorithm A is a function associating one or multiple interpretations to a given data element ϕ.*

$$A : \Phi \to \{0, 1\}^q$$
$$\phi \mapsto (a_1, ..., a_q)$$
$$\text{with } a_k = 1 \text{ if } \phi \text{ has } i_k \in \mathcal{I} \text{ as interpretation}$$
$$\text{and } a_k = 0 \text{ otherwise}$$

We use the following notation, for $k \in \{1, ..., p\}$: $A_j(\phi_k) = (a_{k1}^j, ..., a_{kq}^j)$, as shown in Table 1.

Table 1. Example representation of data, algorithms and interpretations

	A_1				...	A_n			
	i_1	i_2	...	i_q	...	i_1	i_2	...	i_q
ϕ_1	a_{11}^1	a_{12}^1		a_{1q}^1		a_{11}^n	a_{12}^n		a_{1q}^n
ϕ_2		a_{23}^1	...				a_{23}^n	...	
...									
ϕ_p	a_{p1}^1								a_{pq}^n

2.2 Algorithm Ranking

Performance analysis is generally done by ranking algorithms with respect to their results on ground truth data. In order to correctly establish the claims made in this paper, we need to formalise the notion of ranking order of algorithms with respect to a given ground truth.

Definition 3 (Ranking preorder). *A ranking preorder is expressed with respect to a ground truth Ω, and is defined for set of algorithms $\mathbf{A}$, a data set Φ and a set of interpretations $\mathcal{I}$.*

We note $\prec_\Omega$ a preorder on $\mathbf{A}$ such that $A_1 \prec_\Omega A_2$ iff

$$\left| \{(k, l) | a_{k,l}^1 = \Omega(\phi_k, i_l)\} \right| \leq \left| \{(k, l) | a_{k,l}^2 = \Omega(\phi_k, i_l)\} \right|$$

In other terms, algorithms are compared with respect to the cardinality of their agreement with the ground truth.

3   Performance Metrics on Flawless Ground Truth

Comparing algorithms in the presence of perfectly reliable ground truth is what is usually practiced, and does not require extensive statistical approaches, as we recall here. Assuming Ω represents a 100% reliable ground truth, Table 2 shows an example of algorithm outputs for a set of data items.

Table 2. Example of algorithms performing against a perfect ground truth Ω

	A_1				A_2				A_3				Ω			
	i_1	i_2	i_3	i_4	i_1	i_2	i_3	i_4	i_1	i_2	i_3	i_4	i_1	i_2	i_3	i_4
ϕ_1	0	1	0	1	0	1	1	1	0	1	0	1	0	1	0	1
ϕ_2	0	0	1	0	0	0	0	1	1	0	0	1	0	0	0	1
ϕ_3	0	1	1	0	0	1	1	0	0	1	0	0	0	1	1	0
ϕ_4	0	1	1	0	0	1	0	0	1	1	0	0	0	1	0	0
ϕ_5	1	0	0	0	1	0	0	0	1	1	0	0	1	0	0	0

Following the formalism in Definition 3 the most straightforward approach for ranking is to compute the percentage of good answers of each algorithm and to rank them accordingly.

The proportion of correct answers for algorithm A_j is:

$$\tau_{A_j} = \frac{\sum_{\substack{k\in\{1,...,p\} \\ l\in\{1,...,q\}}} \delta_{a^j_{k,l},\Omega(\phi_k,i_l)}}{pq} \tag{1}$$

$$\text{where} \quad \delta_{i,j} = \begin{cases} 1 \text{ if } i = j \\ 0 \text{ if } i \neq j \end{cases} \tag{2}$$

Using τ_{A_j} we can instantiate the algorithm ranking above such that $A_i \prec_\Omega A_j$ iff $\tau_{A_i} <= \tau_{A_j}$ (the better ranked algorithms are on the right, the less ranked on the left).

Applied to the data in Table 2, we obtain $\tau_{A_1} = 0.85$, $\tau_{A_2} = 0.95$, $\tau_{A_3} = 0.8$ and therefore $A_3 \prec_\Omega A_1 \prec_\Omega A_2$.

4   Performance Metrics on Flawed Ground Truth

As we have shown in [5] it is virtually impossible to obtain "error-free" ground truth. We therefore assume Ω contains a proportion of incorrect data. We also assume this proportion is bound by a known value $\varepsilon \in [0, 1]$.

4.1   General Approach

We would like to know how reliable the ranking of a set of algorithms is when it is based on a ground truth that is reliable up to ε. In order to achieve this, let $\overline{\Omega}$ be the absolute ground truth, to which we have no access other than its approximation Ω_ε.

In other terms,

$$\frac{\left|\left\{(\phi, i) \in \Phi \times \mathcal{I} \mid \Omega_\varepsilon(\phi, i) \neq \overline{\Omega}(\phi, i) \right\}\right|}{|\Phi|\,|\mathcal{I}|} \leq \varepsilon$$

Given Ω_ε we can use Definition 3 to define $\prec_{\Omega_\varepsilon}$. The question is whether it is possible to determine if this ranking is a reliable approximation of $\prec_{\overline{\Omega}}$ to which we have no access.

The rest of this paper will address the various probabilistic approaches that will allow us to quantify this difference.

4.2   Notations

In order to develop probabilistic methods, we define the following random variables:

For a given ground truth Ω, an algorithm A_j with $j \in \{1, ..., n\}$, $k \in \{1, ..., p\}$ and $l \in \{1, ..., q\}$, the random variable $X_{k,l}^{\Omega,j}$ expresses whether algorithm A_j correctly interprets ϕ_k as i_l.

This entails that

$$X_{k,l}^{\Omega,j} = \begin{cases} 1 \text{ if } A_j(\phi_k)|_l = \Omega(\phi_k, i_l) \\ 0 \text{ otherwise} \end{cases}$$

which can be expressed also as

$$X_{k,l}^{\Omega,j} = \begin{cases} 1 \text{ if } a_{kl}^j = \Omega(\phi_k, i_l) \\ 0 \text{ otherwise} \end{cases}$$

the realisations of which will be noted as $x_{k,l}^{\Omega,j}$.

The associated probabilities will be noted as

$$\mathbf{P}\left(X_{k,l}^{\Omega,j} = 1\right) = p_{k,l}^{\Omega,j}$$

and

$$\mathbf{P}\left(X_{k,l}^{\Omega,j} = 0\right) = 1 - p_{k,l}^{\Omega,j}$$

with $p_{k,l}^j \in [0, 1]$ $\forall i, j, k$.

5   Simplified Approach Using Two Algorithms

Given the impossibility of using χ^2 multinomial adequacy testing (since it requires knowledge on $\overline{\Omega}$, which we don't have), we have tried to formally and numerically derive statistics on simplified data. In this section we restrict ourselves to two algorithms and one single possible interpretation per algorithm. This will allow us to establish a first category of statistical tests.

	A_1	A_2	Ω_ε	$\overline{\Omega}$
	i	i	i	i
ϕ_1	0	1	0	$x_1^{\overline{\Omega}}$
ϕ_2	0	1	0	$x_2^{\overline{\Omega}}$
ϕ_3	0	1	0	$x_3^{\overline{\Omega}}$
ϕ_4	0	1	0	$x_4^{\overline{\Omega}}$

5.1   Working Hypotheses and Notations

We now assume there are only two algorithms A_1 and A_2 to be compared. We are assuming these algorithms are binary classifiers (*i.e.* there is only one possible interpretation: $\mathcal{I} = \{i\}$; algorithms categorize data in `true` or `false`)

Consequently, we denote the set of values of an algorithm over Φ as $\{a_k^j\}$ and the set of corresponding ground truth values as $\Omega_{cvarepsilon}(\phi_k)$. Once again, let $\overline{\Omega}$ be a perfect ground truth, for which we have no a priori knowledge, nor any algorithm ranking. Similarly, Ω_ε is a ground truth for which all values are known, and of which we know that it differs from $\overline{\Omega}$ by at most ε. This allows us to express a ranking order $\prec_{\Omega_\varepsilon}$ between A_1 and A_2.

In order to develop the rest of our rationale, we need to introduce the notion of *divergence* between two algorithms A_1 and A_2:

Definition 4 (Disagreement Set). *Let A_1 and A_2 be two algorithms of which the results to a known ground truth Ω are known. These results are respectively $a_{k,l}^{\Omega,1}$ and $a_{k,l}^{\Omega,2}$ with $k \in \{1, ..., p\}, l \in \{1, ..., q\}$.*

We define the disagreement set between A_1 and A_2 as

$$\mathcal{D}(A_1, A_2) = \left\{ (k, l) \,\middle|\, a_{k,l}^{\Omega,1} \neq a_{k,l}^{\Omega,2} \right\}.$$

We can extend this notation to also express the disagreement between an algorithm and the ground truth, or between ground truths:

$$\mathcal{D}(A_i, \Omega) = \left\{ (k, l) \,\middle|\, a_{k,l}^{\Omega,i} \neq x_{k,l}^{\Omega} \right\}$$

$$\mathcal{D}(\overline{\Omega}, \Omega_\varepsilon) = \left\{ (k, l) \,\middle|\, x_{k,l}^{\overline{\Omega}} \neq x_{k,l}^{\Omega_\varepsilon} \right\}$$

Definition 5 (Agreement Set). *Let A_1 and A_2 be two algorithms of which the results to a known ground truth Ω are known. These results are respectively $a_{k,l}^{\Omega,1}$ and $a_{k,l}^{\Omega,2}$ with $k \in \{1, ..., p\}, l \in \{1, ..., q\}$.*

We define the agreement set between A_1 and A_2 as

$$\mathcal{A}(A_1, A_2) = \left\{ (k, l) \,\middle|\, a_{k,l}^{\Omega,1} = a_{k,l}^{\Omega,2} \right\}.$$

It is straightforward to note that $\mathcal{A}$ and $\mathcal{D}$ are complements of each other:

$$\mathcal{A}(X, Y) = \overline{\mathcal{D}(X, Y)}.$$

Definition 6 (Divergence between two algorithms). *Let A_1 and A_2 be two algorithms. Given their disagreement sets as per Definition 4, we define divergence between A_1 and A_2 as*

$$\mathbf{D}(A_1, A_2) = |\mathcal{D}(A_1, A_2)|.$$

Divergence is equivalent to the Hamming distance between the vectors containing the output values of A_1 and A_2.

As in the case of the disagreement set, this definition can be extended to express the difference of agreement between algorithms and the ground truth, or between ground truths:

$$\mathbf{D}(A_i, \Omega) = |\mathcal{D}(A_i, \Omega)|$$
$$\mathbf{D}(\overline{\Omega}, \Omega_\varepsilon) = |\mathcal{D}(\overline{\Omega}, \Omega)|$$

5.2   Divergence Estimation

It is straightforward to prove that, in the general case, given any ground truth Ω, the following in equations hold:

$$\mathbf{D}(A_1, A_2) \leq \mathbf{D}(A_1, \Omega) + \mathbf{D}(A_2, \Omega) \tag{3}$$
$$\mathbf{D}(A_2, \Omega) - \mathbf{D}(A_1, \Omega) \leq \mathbf{D}(A_1, A_2) \tag{4}$$

Explanation. (3) results from the triangular inequality of the Hamming distance. It can also be explained by the fact that, on binary classifiers, at best, two algorithms disagree with the ground truth on data points on which they disagree with one another. At worst, both algorithms perfectly agree on all data points (even when in disagreement with the ground truth), in which case $\mathbf{D}(A_1, A_2) = 0$.

(4) can be derived from the fact that the difference in disagreement of two algorithms with the ground truth is at worst their disagreement with one another. This can be easily observed from the extreme configurations where either $\mathbf{D}(A_1, A_2) = 0$ (and consequently $\mathbf{D}(A_2, \Omega) = \mathbf{D}(A_1, \Omega)$) or either $\mathbf{D}(A_1, A_2) = \mathbf{D}(A_1, \Omega) + \mathbf{D}(A_2, \Omega)$.

Given the fact that the divergence between $\overline{\Omega}$ and Ω_ε is bounded by $\varepsilon\, p$ we can deduce that

$$\mathbf{D}(A_i, \overline{\Omega}) - \varepsilon\, p \leq \mathbf{D}(A_i, \Omega_\varepsilon) \leq \mathbf{D}(A_i, \overline{\Omega}) + \varepsilon\, p \tag{5}$$

This implies, by combining (3) and (5), that

$$\mathbf{D}(A_1, \overline{\Omega}) \leq \mathbf{D}(A_1, A_2) + \mathbf{D}(A_2, \Omega_\varepsilon) + \varepsilon\, p \tag{6}$$

Similarly, by combining (4) and (5), we get

$$\mathbf{D}(A_1, \overline{\Omega}) \geq \mathbf{D}(A_1, A_2) - \mathbf{D}(A_2, \Omega_\varepsilon) - \varepsilon\, p \tag{7}$$

Therefore, and because of the symmetry of the demonstration, the divergence between any given algorithm with the (unknown) perfect ground truth, is bounded by the (known) disagreement between both algorithms and the assumed error level of the (known) tainted ground truth.

5.3   Estimating the Probability of a Change in Ranking

At this point in the process, we have a tainted ground truth Ω_ε and two algorithms A_1 and A_2, which we can rank using $\prec_{\Omega_\varepsilon}$. The question that arises is that, if we had done the ranking based on $\overline{\Omega}$ (*i.e.* without the ε ground truth error), would the ordering of the two algorithms have changed?

We therefore address the question of whether a change in the value of ε changes the ranking of the algorithms, by formalising it as a probabilistic problem. Let $\mathbf{P}\left(A_1 \prec_{\overline{\Omega}} A_2 \big| A_1 \prec_{\Omega_\varepsilon} A_2\right)$ be the probability that the ranking remains unchanged for ground truth $\overline{\Omega}$ given the ranking for Ω_ε.

Let us consider the specific example where $|\mathbf{D}(A_1, \Omega_\varepsilon) - \mathbf{D}(A_2, \Omega_\varepsilon)| > 2\varepsilon p$ (p being the number of data elements in Φ). In this case, the order $\prec_{\Omega_\varepsilon}$ on A_1 and A_2 will be strictly equivalent to $\prec_{\overline{\Omega}}$.

Indeed, let's assume $A_1 \prec_{\Omega_\varepsilon} A_2$. In the worst case, both A_1 and A_2 agree with Ω_ε on those data where Ω_ε gets it wrong with respect to $\overline{\Omega}$. In that situation, the following holds:

$$\mathcal{D}\left(\overline{\Omega}, \Omega_\varepsilon\right) \subset \mathcal{D}\left(A_1, \overline{\Omega}\right) \cap \mathcal{D}\left(A_2, \overline{\Omega}\right)$$

where, by definition, for the worst case scenario, $\mathbf{D}\left(\overline{\Omega}, \Omega_\varepsilon\right) = p\varepsilon$. Therefore

$$\mathbf{D}(A_1, \overline{\Omega}) = \mathbf{D}(A_1, \Omega_\varepsilon) + p\varepsilon$$

and

$$\mathbf{D}(A_2, \overline{\Omega}) = \mathbf{D}(A_2, \Omega_\varepsilon) - p\varepsilon$$

Since we made the assumption that $A_1 \prec_{\Omega_\varepsilon} A_2$ (and thus $\mathbf{D}(A_1, \Omega_\varepsilon) - \mathbf{D}(A_2, \Omega_\varepsilon) > 0$), we obtain that $\mathbf{D}(A_1, \overline{\Omega}) - \mathbf{D}(A_2, \overline{\Omega}) > 0$, and consequently $A_1 \prec_{\overline{\Omega}} A_2$.

We can therefore conclude that

$$\mathbf{P}\left(A_1 \prec_{\overline{\Omega}} A_2 \big| A_1 \prec_{\Omega_\varepsilon} A_2\right) = 1$$

if $\mathbf{D}(A_2, \Omega_\varepsilon) - \mathbf{D}(A_1, \Omega_\varepsilon) \geq 2\varepsilon p$.

If we consider $\mathcal{A}(A_2, \Omega_\varepsilon)$ the set of values common to A_2 and Ω_ε, and $\mathcal{D}(A_1, \Omega_\varepsilon)$ the set values where A_1 and Ω_ε differ, then

$$\mathbf{P}\left(A_1 \prec_{\overline{\Omega}} A_2 \big| A_1 \prec_{\Omega_\varepsilon} A_2\right) = 1 \qquad \text{if}$$

$$|\mathcal{A}(A_2, \Omega_\varepsilon) \cap \mathcal{D}(A_1, \Omega_\varepsilon)| < \frac{\mathbf{D}(A_2, \Omega_\varepsilon) - \mathbf{D}(A_1, \Omega_\varepsilon)}{2}$$

Explanation. The only case where A_1 could inverse its ranking with respect to A_2 is when there is a sufficiently high number of values in $\mathcal{A}(A_2, \Omega_\varepsilon) \cap \mathcal{D}(A_1, \Omega_\varepsilon)$ for which $\overline{\Omega}$ differs from Ω_ε. We need at least $\frac{\mathbf{D}(A_2,\Omega_\varepsilon) - \mathbf{D}(A_1,\Omega_\varepsilon)}{2}$.

In the general case, one can use a Monte-Carlo simulation [8] in which the values of $\Omega_\varepsilon(\phi_k)$ are changed with a probability of ε. Although there is a fundamental difference between having a strictly bounded ground truth uncertainty of ε and using the same value as the likelihood of individual values being different between $\overline{\Omega}$ and Ω_ε, we can use the approach for estimating $\mathbf{P}\left(A_1 \prec_{\overline{\Omega}} A_2 \mid_{A_1 \prec_{\Omega_\varepsilon} A_2}\right)$. The main reasons are that the high number of iterations of the Monte-Carlo simulation will converge to a Gaussian distribution around ε errors, and that in real situations, ε is usually an approximate guess with an associated Gaussian uncertainty. Furthermore, the closed-form developments in the next section support the numerical simulations obtained here.

Algorithm. Execute the following loop N times (for large values of N)

- all values k in $[1..p]$, change the value of $\Omega_\varepsilon(\phi_k)$ with a probability of ε;
- compute $\mathbf{D}(A_2, \Omega_\varepsilon) - \mathbf{D}(A_1, \Omega_\varepsilon)$;
- if $\mathbf{D}(A_2, \Omega_\varepsilon) - \mathbf{D}(A_1, \Omega_\varepsilon) \geq 0$, increase counter c by 1.

After N iterations $\frac{c}{N}$ yields an approximation of the required probability.

Example. we have used a Matlab implementation of Monte-Carlo on the data in Table 3. In our example $A_1 \prec_{\Omega_\varepsilon} A_2$ and $p = 10$.

Table 3. Simple example of two algorithms performing against binary ground truth.

	A_1	A_2	Ω_ε	$\overline{\Omega}$
	i	i	i	i
ϕ_1	0	0	0	$x_1^{\overline{\Omega}}$
ϕ_2	1	1	1	$x_2^{\overline{\Omega}}$
ϕ_3	1	1	1	$x_3^{\overline{\Omega}}$
ϕ_4	1	0	0	$x_4^{\overline{\Omega}}$
ϕ_5	1	0	0	$x_5^{\overline{\Omega}}$
ϕ_6	0	1	1	$x_6^{\overline{\Omega}}$
ϕ_7	0	1	0	$x_7^{\overline{\Omega}}$
ϕ_8	0	0	1	$x_8^{\overline{\Omega}}$
ϕ_9	0	0	1	$x_9^{\overline{\Omega}}$
ϕ_{10}	1	1	0	$x_{10}^{\overline{\Omega}}$

With $N = 10^5$ tests and a confidence level of 95% we obtain:

- $\varepsilon = 0.5$: $\mathbf{P}(A_1 \prec_{\overline{\Omega}} A_2) = 0.3135 \pm 0.002876$
- $\varepsilon = 0.2$: $\mathbf{P}(A_1 \prec_{\overline{\Omega}} A_2) = 0.5893 \pm 0.003049$
- $\varepsilon = 0.1$: $\mathbf{P}(A_1 \prec_{\overline{\Omega}} A_2) = 0.7517 \pm 0.002677$
- $\varepsilon = 0$: as expected $\mathbf{P}(A_1 \prec_{\overline{\Omega}} A_2) = 1$

5.4   Formal Approach

It is to be noted that the previous Monte-Carlo based solution is a mere convenience, and that a formal solution can be derived as well.

Indeed, one can make the following observations:

1. Given the fact that Ω_ε differs from $\overline{\Omega}$ by ε, the probability of $\Omega_\varepsilon\,(\phi_i)$ differing from $\overline{\Omega}\,(\phi_i)$, expressed as $\mathbf{P}\left(x_i^{\overline{\Omega}} \neq x_i^{\Omega_\varepsilon}\right)$, can be considered to be following a Bernoulli law of parameter ε. (This is exactly what is expressed by the probability of change in the above Monte-Carlo approach)
2. We are trying to measure the impact of a disagreement between Ω_ε and $\overline{\Omega}$ on the ranking between A_1 and A_2. For each ϕ_i where A_1 and A_2 are in agreement (regardless whether they agree or not with Ω_ε) a change in $\Omega_\varepsilon\,(\phi_i)$ is not going to affect the ranking $A_1 \prec_{\Omega_\varepsilon} A_2$ since both will be affected in the same sense.
As a consequence, $\mathbf{P}\,(A_1 \prec_{\overline{\Omega}} A_2)$ only depends on the probability of Ω_ε being in disagreement with $\overline{\Omega}$ on only those ϕ_i where A_1 disagrees with A_2.

Based on these observations, and using the same notations as before, we can compute the probability of $\mathbf{P}\,(A_1 \prec_{\overline{\Omega}} A_2)$ as follows.

Let $\mathcal{D}_{A_1}$ (resp. $\mathcal{D}_{A_2}$) be the subset of $\mathcal{D}\,(A_1, A_2)$ where A_1 (resp. A_2) is in agreement with Ω_ε while being in disagreement with A_2 (resp. A_1).

$$\mathcal{D}_{A_1} = \mathcal{D}\,(A_1, A_2) \cap \mathcal{A}\,(A_1, \Omega_\varepsilon)$$

$$\mathcal{D}_{A_2} = \mathcal{D}\,(A_1, A_2) \cap \mathcal{A}\,(A_2, \Omega_\varepsilon)$$

Since we are only considering two algorithms, and given observation 2 above, this is equivalent to

$$\mathcal{D}_{A_1} = \mathcal{D}\,(A_1, A_2) - \mathcal{D}\,(A_2, \Omega_\varepsilon)$$

$$\mathcal{D}_{A_2} = \mathcal{D}\,(A_1, A_2) - \mathcal{D}\,(A_1, \Omega_\varepsilon)$$

It is straightforward to prove that $\mathcal{D}_{A_1} \cap \mathcal{D}_{A_2} = \emptyset$ and that $A_1 \prec_{\Omega_\varepsilon} A_2$ iff $\mathbf{D}_{A_1} \leq \mathbf{D}_{A_2}$ (where $\mathbf{D}$ expresses the cardinality of $\mathcal{D}$).

Furthermore, $\mathcal{D}_{A_1} \cap \mathcal{D}_{A_2} = \emptyset$ implies that $\mathbf{D}_{A_2} = \mathbf{D}\,(A_1, A_2) - \mathbf{D}_{A_1}$ and therefore that

$$A_1 \prec_{\Omega_\varepsilon} A_2 \; iff \; \mathbf{D}_{A_1} \leq \frac{\mathbf{D}\,(A_1, A_2)}{2}. \tag{8}$$

$\mathbf{D}\,(A_1, A_2)$ is independent from Ω. Consequently one can conclude that $\mathbf{P}\,(A_1 \prec_{\overline{\Omega}} A_2)$ corresponds to the probability of

$$D = \mathbf{D}_{A_1} - \frac{\mathbf{D}\,(A_1, A_2)}{2}$$

not changing signs.

Without loss of generality and because of the symmetry of the problem, we can assume that the numbering of A_1 and A_2 is chosen such that $A_1 \prec_{\Omega_\varepsilon} A_2$, and therefore $\mathbf{D}_{A_1} \leq \mathbf{D}_{A_2}$ and thus $D < 0$.

D will switch signs if at least $\hat{D} = \frac{D(A_1, A_2)}{2} - \mathbf{D}_{A_1}$ events in $\mathcal{D}_{A_2}$ are in disagreement with $\overline{\Omega}$ (and if none of those in $\mathcal{D}_{A_1}$ are). Given that our events are following a Bernouli law of parameter ε, the probability of having at least $\hat{D}$ events (and thus D switching signs) is

$$\sum_{i=\hat{D}}^{\mathbf{D}_{A_2}} \binom{\mathbf{D}_{A_2}}{i} \varepsilon^i (1-\varepsilon)^{\mathbf{D}_{A_2}-i} = \sum_{i=\hat{D}}^{\mathbf{D}_{A_2}} \mathcal{B}(\mathbf{D}_{A_2}, i). \tag{9}$$

This probability is conditioned by the fact that all of the events of $\mathcal{D}_{A_1}$ are in agreement with $\overline{\Omega}$. If k events of $\mathcal{D}_{A_1}$ are in disagreement with $\overline{\Omega}$, then the above probability becomes

$$\sum_{i=\hat{D}+k}^{\mathbf{D}_{A_2}} \mathcal{B}(\mathbf{D}_{A_2}, i). \tag{10}$$

Therefore, the global probability covering all cases, of D switching signs is

$$\mathbf{P}_{\text{switch}} = \sum_{k=0}^{\mathbf{D}_{A_1}} \mathcal{B}(\mathbf{D}_{A_1}, k) \sum_{i=\hat{D}+k}^{\mathbf{D}_{A_2}} \mathcal{B}(\mathbf{D}_{A_2}, i). \tag{11}$$

Finally, since we are looking for the probability of the initial ranking remaining unchanged, we obtain that

$$\mathbf{P}\left(A_1 \prec_{\overline{\Omega}} A_2 \,\middle|\, A_1 \prec_{\Omega_\varepsilon} A_2\right) = 1 - \mathbf{P}_{\text{switch}} \tag{12}$$

Numerical Example. Using the data in Table 3, we observe that $A_1 \prec_{\Omega_\varepsilon} A_2$. Furthermore,

$$\mathcal{D}(A_1, A_2) = \{\phi_4, \phi_5, \phi_6, \phi_7\}$$

$$\mathcal{A}(A_1, \Omega_\varepsilon) = \{\phi_1, \phi_2, \phi_3, \phi_7\} \qquad \mathcal{A}(A_2, \Omega_\varepsilon) = \{\phi_1, \phi_2, \phi_3, \phi_4, \phi_5, \phi_6\}$$
$$\mathcal{D}_{A_1} = \{\phi_7\} \qquad\qquad \mathcal{D}_{A_2} = \{\phi_4, \phi_5, \phi_6\}$$

The other parameters we observe from the data are: $\mathbf{D}_{A_1} = 1$, $\mathbf{D}_{A_2} = 3$ and $\hat{D} = 1$. We can therefore rewrite Eq. 12 as

$$\mathbf{P}(A_1 \prec_{\overline{\Omega}} A_2) = 1 - \sum_{k=0}^{1} \binom{1}{k} \varepsilon^k (1-\varepsilon)^{1-k} \sum_{i=1+k}^{3} \binom{3}{i} \varepsilon^i (1-\varepsilon)^{3-i} \tag{13}$$

$$= 1 - \left((1-\varepsilon)\left(3\varepsilon(1-\varepsilon)^2 + 3\varepsilon^2(1-\varepsilon) + \varepsilon^3\right) + \varepsilon\left(3\varepsilon^2(1-\varepsilon) + \varepsilon^3\right)\right)$$
$$= 1 - \varepsilon\left(3 - 6\varepsilon + 7\varepsilon^2 - 3\varepsilon^4\right)$$

We obtain:

- $\varepsilon = 0.5$: $\mathbf{P}(A_1 \prec_{\overline{\Omega}} A_2) = 0.313$
- $\varepsilon = 0.2$: $\mathbf{P}(A_1 \prec_{\overline{\Omega}} A_2) = 0.589$
- $\varepsilon = 0.1$: $\mathbf{P}(A_1 \prec_{\overline{\Omega}} A_2) = 0.753$
- $\varepsilon = 0$: as expected $\mathbf{P}(A_1 \prec_{\overline{\Omega}} A_2) = 1$

Thus confirming the previously obtained Monte-Carlo estimates.

6   Extension to Multiple Interpretations and Confidence Levels

Until now, we have been considering two algorithms expressing boolean values for a single interpretation. We are still considering two algorithms but expressing confidence values for multiple possible interpretations. In order to handle this case, we are going to use the Kullback-Leibler divergence [4]. The Kullback-Leibler divergence is a dissimilarity measure between two probability distributions P and Q, where P represents a series of observations, or a precisely computed probability distribution, and Q a model or an approximation of P.

Definition 7 (Kullback-Leibler Divergence). *Let P and Q be two probability distributions. The Kullback-Leibler distribution of Q with respect to P is defined by*

$$D_{KL}(P||Q) = \sum_i P(i)\, ln\left(\frac{P(i)}{Q(i)}\right)$$

Note: $D_{KL}(P||Q) = D_{KL}(Q||P) = 0$ *iff* $P = Q$.

6.1   Application to Ranking Evaluation

In order to apply Kullback-Leibler to our case, we need probability distributions. We therefore need to reformulate our problem, and restrict it to some specific cases.

Hypotheses.

1. We are still considering two algorithms only.
2. Multiple interpretations are possible (*i.e.* $q \geq 1$).
3. Ground Truth attributes only one interpretation to each data element.
4. Algorithms return a confidence value in $[0..1]$ per possible interpretation for each data element.

We therefore need to redefine the formal concept of an algorithm initially given in Definition 2 as follows:

Definition 8 (Algorithm). *An algorithm A is a function associating a confidence value for one or multiple interpretations to a given data element ϕ.*

$$A : \Phi \rightarrow [0..1]^q$$
$$\phi \mapsto (a_1, ..., a_q)$$
$$with \ \sum_{l=1}^{q} a_l = 1$$

As such, the interpretation confidence of a given data element can be assimilated to a probability distribution.

For a given ground truth Ω and a data element ϕ_k we obtain the following Kullback-Leibler distribution:

$$D_{KL} \left(A_i \left(\phi_k \right) || \Omega \right) = \sum_{l=1}^{q} a_{kl}^j \ ln \left(\frac{a_{kl}^j}{\Omega(\phi_k, i_l)} \right)$$

Application. Let A_1 and A_2 be two algorithms to compare. Let $\overline{\Omega}$ be an ideal ground truth of which we have no precise knowledge. Let Ω_ε be a known ground truth, differing from $\overline{\Omega}$ by ε.

First, we establish the ranking between A_1 and A_2 by using the sum of the Kullback-Leibler divergence for all data elements.

$$\mathbf{D} \left(A_i, \Omega_\varepsilon \right) = \sum_{k=1}^{p} D_{KL} \left(A_i \left(\phi_k \right) || \Omega_\varepsilon \right)$$

We can then apply the same definitions and techniques as in the previous sections. $A_1 \prec_{\Omega_\varepsilon} A_2$ *iff* $\mathbf{D} \left(A_1, \Omega_\varepsilon \right) >= \mathbf{D} \left(A_2, \Omega_\varepsilon \right)$ or, in other terms, *iff*

$$\sum_{k=1}^{p} D_{KL}(A_1(\phi_k) || \Omega_\varepsilon) \geq \sum_{k=1}^{p} D_{KL}(A_2(\phi_k) || \Omega_\varepsilon)$$

$\mathbf{P} \left(A_1 \prec_{\Omega} A_2 \big|_{A_1 \prec_{\Omega_\varepsilon} A_2} \right)$ can now be computed following the same technique as described previously, by replacing the formal divergence formulae with a Monte-Carlo simulation.

Numerical Example. Using the data in Table 4, with $N = 10^5$ and a 95% confidence we obtain:

- $\varepsilon = 0.5$: $\mathbf{P}(A_1 \prec_{\Omega} A_2) = 0.6663 \pm 0.0029$
- $\varepsilon = 0.4$: $\mathbf{P}(A_1 \prec_{\Omega} A_2) = 0.7353 \pm 0.0027$
- $\varepsilon = 0.2$: $\mathbf{P}(A_1 \prec_{\Omega} A_2) = 0.8665 \pm 0.0021$

Table 4. Numerical example for Kullback-Leibler divergence-based ranking evaluation

	A_1				A_2				Ω_ε			
	i_1	i_2	i_3	i_4	i_1	i_2	i_3	i_4	i_1	i_2	i_3	i_4
ϕ_1	0.3	0.1	0.4	0	0.2	0.6	0.2	0	1	0	0	1
ϕ_2	0.5	0.2	0.1	0.2	0	0.1	0.8	0.1	0	0	1	0
ϕ_3	0.6	0.2	0.1	0.1	0.5	0.3	0.1	0.1	1	0	0	0
ϕ_4	0.4	0.2	0.4	0	0.4	0.3	0.2	0.1	0	1	0	0
ϕ_5	0.1	0.8	0.1	0	0.9	0.1	0	0	1	0	0	0
ϕ_5	0.6	0.3	0	0.1	0.2	0.2	0.2	0.4	0	0	0	1

7 Conclusion and Perspectives

In this paper we have explored various methods for evaluating algorithm performances with respect to an unreliable ground truth, by expressing the probability that the observed ranking be modified given an error boundary estimate on the ground truth quality.

Our models are able to express the probability of the ranking between two algorithms to flip in presence of a given estimated uncertainty on the ground truth and in the absence of any knowledge of the absolute, untainted ground truth. We have expressed this probability formally in the case of binary interpretation algorithms, and validated it with a Monte-Carlo simulation. We have also formalised the possibility of using Kullback-Leibler divergence in the case of non-binary interpretation algorithms when the interpretations are associated with probability values.

The current limitation of our models is that they yet need to be extended to the ranking of multiple algorithms ($n > 2$) on the one hand, and that the array of possible interpretations be expanded beyond simple binary or probabilistic interpretations, on the other. These theoretical results (although formally proven) also need to be experimentally assessed on real data [6]. Unfortunately, most current published benchmark results only publish precision and recall curves and values, while our methods require access to the complete experimental result set.

Further work will also focus on extending the current conclusions and techniques to simple precision and recall curves.

References

1. Al-Khaffaf, H.S.M., Talib, A.Z., Osman, M.A., Wong, P.L.: GREC'09 Arc Segmentation Contest: Performance Evaluation on Old Documents. In: Ogier, J.-M., Liu, W., Lladós, J. (eds.) GREC 2009. LNCS, vol. 6020, pp. 251–259. Springer, Heidelberg (2010). doi:10.1007/978-3-642-13728-0_23

2. Al-Khaffaf, H.S.M., Talib, A.Z., Osman, M.A.: Final report of GREC'11 arc segmentation contest: performance evaluation on multi-resolution scanned documents. In: Kwon, Y.-B., Ogier, J.-M. (eds.) GREC 2011. LNCS, vol. 7423, pp. 187–197. Springer, Heidelberg (2013). doi:10.1007/978-3-642-36824-0_18
3. Al-Khaffaf, H.S.M., Talib, A.Z., Osman, M.A., Wong, P.L.: GREC'09 arc segmentation contest: performance evaluation on old documents. In: Ogier, J.-M., Liu, W., Lladós, J. (eds.) GREC 2009. LNCS, vol. 6020, pp. 251–259. Springer, Heidelberg (2010). doi:10.1007/978-3-642-13728-0_23
4. Kullback, S., Leibler, R.A.: On information and sufficiency. Ann. Math. Statist. **22**(1), 79–86 (1951). http://dx.doi.org/10.1214/aoms/1177729694
5. Lamiroy, B.: Interpretation, evaluation and the semantic gap.. what if we were on a side-track? In: Lamiroy, B., Ogier, J.-M. (eds.) GREC 2013. LNCS, vol. 8746, pp. 221–233. Springer, Heidelberg (2014). doi:10.1007/978-3-662-44854-0_17
6. Lamiroy, B., Sun, T.: Computing precision and recall with missing or uncertain ground truth. In: Kwon, Y.-B., Ogier, J.-M. (eds.) GREC 2011. LNCS, vol. 7423, pp. 149–162. Springer, Heidelberg (2013). doi:10.1007/978-3-642-36824-0_15
7. Wenyin, L.: The third report of the arc segmentation contest. In: Liu, W., Lladós, J. (eds.) GREC 2005. LNCS, vol. 3926, pp. 358–361. Springer, Heidelberg (2006). doi:10.1007/11767978_32
8. Metropolis, N., Ulam, S.M.: The Monte Carlo method. J. Am. Stat. Assoc. **44**(247), 335–341 (1949). http://dx.doi.org/10.2307/2280232

Recognition and Content Analysis

Migrating the Classical Pen-and-Paper Based Conceptual Sketching of Architecture Plans Towards Computer Tools - Prototype Design and Evaluation

Johannes Bayer[1], Syed Saqib Bukhari[1(✉)], Christoph Langenhan[2],
Marcus Liwicki[3], Klaus-Dieter Althoff[1], Frank Petzold[2], and Andreas Dengel[1]

[1] German Research Center for Artificial Intelligence, Kaiserslautern, Germany
{johannes.bayer,saqib.bukhari,klaus-dieter.althoff,
andreas.dengel}@dfki.de
[2] Techniche Universität München, Munich, Germany
{langenhan,petzold}@tum.de
[3] Kaiserslautern University, Kaiserslautern, Germany
liwicki@cs.uni-kl.de

Abstract. While computer-based design tools are widely used in ⁎architecure during late design phases for creating final floor plans, early design phases usually still take place in a traditional manner, using pen, paper and scissors. At the beginning of these phases, there is often only a rough idea of how a building should look like. Viewing existing floorplans of similar buildings can help an architect in his/her creative work, but searching for those plans manually is very time-consuming. Automated tools for searching similar floor plans could help to lower the amount of time needed for such investigations tremendously. In order to employ such search mechanisms, proper user interfaces are needed that fit to the architect's working process. These interfaces should be useable easily and naturally, requiring less initial training. They should be capable of creating search requests that can be processed by the attached search mechanism. In this article, we describe two different user interfaces to serve this purpose. We describe their structures and interaction principles. Afterwards we show their general usability and user acceptance by the means of a users study.

Keywords: Conceptual design phase · Architectural working method · Metis webUI · TouchTect

1 Introduction

In the early stages of the design process, the conceptual idea of the envisaged building and its design parameters is still vague and incomplete. While the built environment, the end product of this design process, can be represented concretely in the form of drawings or computer models, the initial design idea

B. Lamiroy and R. Dueire Lins (Eds.): GREC 2015, LNCS 9657, pp. 47–59, 2017.
DOI: 10.1007/978-3-319-52159-6_4

can usually only be formulated abstractly, for example as schematic functional descriptions or as topological constellations of spaces and or of relative proportions. A method that is therefore commonly used in the early design phases is to consult reference projects: by drawing on analogies from existing buildings or architectural designs, the designer can verify his or her ideas, identify relevant design parameters or explore new directions and possibilities. As part of a research project (referred as Metis), funded by the German Research Foundation (DFG), innovative research methods are being developed to support design actions in the conceptual design phase. Approaches have been developed for the IT-support and linking of two key design strategies that architects use when developing ideas: functional and conceptual drawings and the use of reference material. Therefore a semantic fingerprint was proposed as a means of characterising a building in much the same way as a fingerprint identifies a person [4]. This same approach can also be used as a mean of formulating architectural situations and in turn for identifying semantic similarities. The semantic fingerprint attempts to address the primary problem of the vague and incomplete nature of design ideas, creating a way of identifying analogous reference examples of existing buildings or building designs. By drawing on analogies from existing buildings or architectural designs, the designer can verify his or her ideas, identify relevant design parameters or explore new directions and possibilities. The core aims of the Metis research project are:

- To find ways of accessing implicit knowledge contained in reference projects
- To formulate knowledge in the form of graphs
- To develop methods and models for retrieving specified formal structures
- To develop a way to specify and to search and retrieve spatial configurations

Working with references is an established methodology in the architectural design process. Functional diagrams and sketches are to formulate initial ideas, for example. In the research project Metis the focus is to formulate queries to the computer, which is the basis for the search in a digital building repository called "ar:searchbox" (located at TU Munich). The presented user study examines the extent to which existing prototypes to support the formulation of queries with freehand sketches and functional diagrams can be performed.

However, even till today, architects feel comfortable with pen-and-paper based conceptual sketching. So, as a starting point, a migration from pen-and-paper to simple computer tools is required, in order to achieve further benefits, that are stated as the aims of the project.

In this article, we describe two different graphical user interfaces, that can be used by architects in conceptual design sketching. We first describe the structures and interaction principles of both the presented GUIs. Afterwards we show their general usability and user acceptance by the means of a users study.

The paper is organized as follows. Section 2 describes the classical style of conceptual sketching. Section 3 presents the two different graphics user interfaces for migrating the classical sketching style towards computer tools. Section 4 describes the experimental setup for user study. Section 5 presents the result of the user study and Sect. 7.

2   Classical Style of Conceptual Sketching

In the design process of architecture various tools and strategies are used. "Every design tool serves the perception of external circumstances (capturing and) as well as the expression of imaginations (the imprinting of inner design concepts onto a physical medium). Every design tool can either be descriptive (which means depicting, describing the given), or prescriptive (which means designing, for displaying something new)" [2]. However, certain tools are more suitable as presentation tool (CAD program or drawing board) and others as thinking tool (freehand drawing or reference). Thinking tools support the rapid materialization of thoughts to perceive and evaluate the materialized fragments of design ideas. The knowledge gained flow into the thought process, and can be described as a kind circular dialogue, as shown in Fig. 1, of the designer with the design tool. Buxton writes: "If you want to get the most out of a sketch, you need to leave big enough holes" [1].

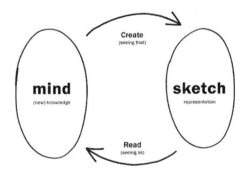

Fig. 1. Sketch of a dialogue with a sketch.

Thinking tools are for example, writing texts, the making of freehand drawings and the use of references as "[...] concrete evidence in support of prediction [...]" [3]. In the early design stages freehand drawings are often used because it is a familiar, efficient and natural way to quickly express and analyze ideas. Freehand drawings can be used to represent unfinished or fragmentary ideas and thoughts, because usually there is still no precise idea of the final result. Gänshirt writes: "The simplicity of the tool enforces to reduce to the essential" [2].

3   Graphical User Interfaces for Conceptual Sketching

We have developed two different digital tools for supporting architects during early design phases: TouchTect and the Metis WebUI.

3.1 TouchTect

Touchtect 2.0 is a Windows application which can be used to query data on multiple web services. It connects to GmlMatcher, Mediatum, Neo4j, the unified-query-service and the bim-server. The application aims at letting this multiple databases look like one. Pen-based interaction on tablet computers and multi-touch tables is supported and give the architect the freedom of expressing ideas intuitively.

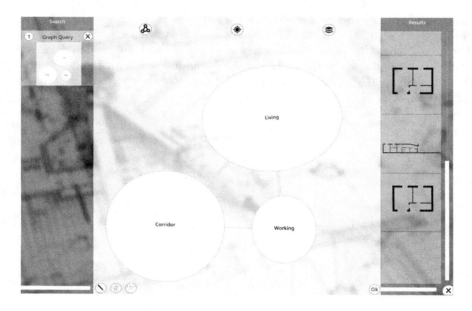

Fig. 2. Screenshot of the TouchTect UI.

In the middle, the free hand sketching canvas support the architect by let him draw a design idea in a schematic way. On the left hand side different queries can be combined like searching for a building that exists in a certain city or one that fits the hand drawing and has seven rooms. On the right hand side a preview of the search results is shown in the form of floor plans. By selecting a result, additional information like pictures and 3D visualisation of the building can be examined.

3.2 Metis WebUI

The Metis WebUI is a tool that was inspired by a working method called *room schedule* or *space allocation plan*. The idea of a room schedule in architecture is that a set of rooms is given as a requirement for a building (e.g. as a list). Some of these rooms may have a specific size, function, and there may be requirements for neighborhoods of rooms as well as passages between rooms. It is a more abstract working method than direct sketching but it also used in practice, where a room schedule is usually coming in form of a list of requirements from the customer. Since the architect may have more concrete ideas for some room layouts and rather rough imaginations about other rooms, we tried to build a tool that supports multiple abstraction levels allowing for specifying (and respecifying) design aspects as concrete or abstract as desired by the user.

Figure 3 shows a screenshot of the Metis WebUI. The Metis WebUI runs inside a standard web browser and was entirely written in HTML5/Javascript. It allows for combining abstract rooms i.e. rooms that have no specified wall layout yet (displayed by bubbles) and rooms with concrete wall layouts. Within the abstract mode (also reffered to as bubble mode), already the room's size and function can be set, and the room can be interconnected by neighborhood links (displayed as single lines) and passage links (displayed as double lines). Neighborhood links symbolizes that two rooms are located next to each other (they share a wall) and passage link just means that a person can physically move from one room to another, either by a door or by a doorless passage. If the user has a concrete wall layout in his mind, he can draw the shape of the room and afterwards place windows and doors into the room's walls. The connections to a room are adopted as they stand when the room is changed from bubble mode to a concrete room layout. Doors and windows can be resized and moved along the walls on which they were created. Multiple doors/windows per wall are allowed. Except for one button that creates new rooms and a few helper functions, the interface is entirely controlled by radial menus. Single rooms can be moved by mouse and doors can be connected to other rooms or doors by

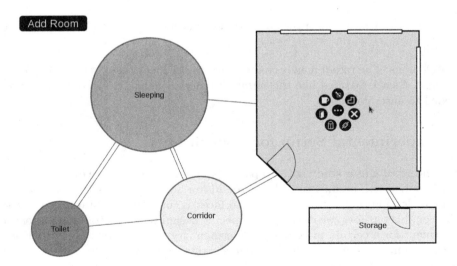

Fig. 3. Screenshot of Metis WebUI showing both rooms with concrete layout and rooms in bubble mode.

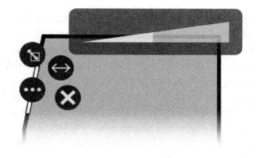

(a) Radial Menu for Doors.   (b) Radial Menu for Windows. Nearby the move button, a slider for adjusting the position of the window is displayed.

(c) Radial Menu for Passage/Neigborhood Links.   (d) Radial Menu for rooms.

Fig. 4. Screenshots of the different radial menus of the Metis WebUI.

passage links. The radial menus change with the element they focus, as depicted in Fig. 4. Smart features like the *autolink* function helps to speed up the time needed to enter concepts.

4 Experimental Setup for User Study

We conducted a user study with 15 participants in which we have examined how well humans with architectural background are able to express their ideas in a fictional design process with our user interfaces as compared to established methods. For this purpose, we developed a specific design scenario: to design a rental apartment for a certain price in a big German city from scratch, no restrictions on the ground plan were given. The participants were asked to first create some free-style drawings and then to develop a design based on a space allocation plan. Every task had initially to be done on paper as established method and directly afterwards on one of our user interfaces (TouchTect for the free-style drawing,

Metis WebUI for the space allocation plan). The participants had no specific time limit and were rudimentary guided by the study's supervisors. For analysis purposes, the participants were videotaped and asked to fill out a questionnaire. Nearly all of the participants were affiliated with TU Munich and were therefore aware of the Metis projects content. Nevertheless, none of the participants had used the prototypes before the study. With one exception all of the participants are familiar with typical architectural software.

5   Analysis of User Study

One way of evaluating the quality of a user interface is to assess its effectiveness (to what degree was the user capable of archiving his goals at all), its efficiency (how much resources - usually time - did the user need to archive his goals) and its user's satisfaction (to what degree did the user "like" the interface). In order to measure these categories, we conducted a user study in which the participants were asked to perform a open draft task (a situation that fits best to the purpose of the developed prototypes). This experimental design comes with the problem that the final layouts drafted by the participants are not fixed, but depend on their ideas. We could have designed the experiment in a way that the participants should only copy a given floorplan, what would have made the assessment of the effectiveness more easy, but such a task would contradict the intention of the prototypes. But since the participants were asked to first do their drafts on paper and then use the examined prototypes, they usually just copied their previous work. In order to assess how much the traditional working methods are used by the participants, we asked them whether or not they have used them before the study (Fig. 5). As expected, the vast majority was familiar with the traditional, examined methods.

In order to assess the user's effectiveness, we asked the participants to what degree the constructs displayed on the interface matched their imaginations and to what degree they could express their ideas by using the interfaces

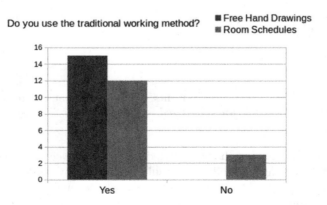

Fig. 5. Use of the traditional working methods by the participants.

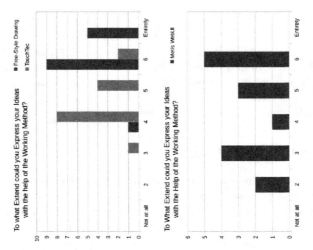

(a) Expressiveness compari-(b) Expressiveness of the
son between Touchtect and Metis WebUI.
Free-Style drawings.

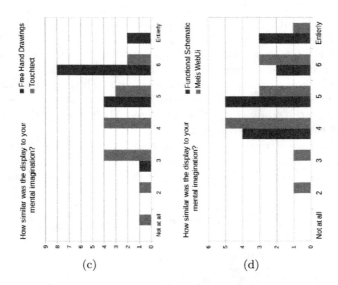

(c) (d)

Fig. 6. Different effectiveness measurements. Please note that the terms functional
schematic and room schedule are considered to be equal here.

(Fig. 6a, b, c and d). Although there were differences between our interfaces and
the traditional working methods, the results were roughly comparable. For the
majority of user, our tools appeared to be at least reasonalbe useable.

We asked a couple of questions that can't be entirely classified into one of the
tree mentioned categories, but the following questions are somewhere between

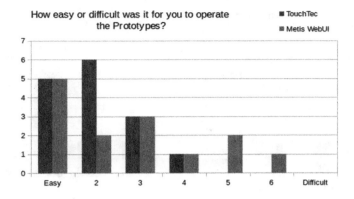

Fig. 7. Difficulty for the users to handle the interfaces.

user's satisfaction and efficiency: We asked the participants how difficult it was to handle the prototypes (see Fig. 7) and how exhausting they perceived the work with the examined interfaces (see Fig. 8). We asked how obstructive the use of mouse and keyboard (Metis WebUI) or the digital pen (TouchTect) was for them (see Fig. 9). We also asked the amount of "perceived time" until the display of the interfaces met the imaginations of the users (Fig. 10a and b). For these questions, the results for our interfaces were pretty similar to the traditional working methods. In other words, handling our prototypes appeared not much more time-consuming or exhausting than sketching on normal paper. In order to assess the user's satisfaction, we asked the participants to what degree they can imagine to use the tools in real life (since this question appears suggestive afterwards, we skip the results here).

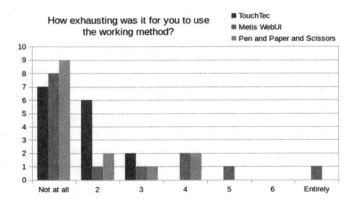

Fig. 8. Exhaustion comparison between the examined interfaces and the classical working methods.

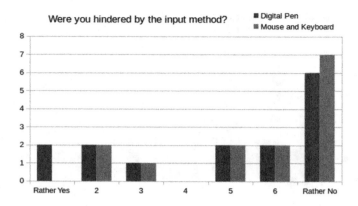

Fig. 9. Comparison of obstruction of different input methods.

6   Improvements of GUI Based on User Feedback

Even before conducting and analysing the user study, several issues were spotted by the domain experts and programmers: In order to create useful search queries, more freedom in entering the concepts is helpfull, but too much freedom may distract the user: In the Metis WebUI, a user may draw passage connections between two rooms, two doors and as well as room and door. The idea behind this freedom was that passage connections between two rooms are more abstract than passage connections between doors. But as expected, some users didn't understand what the difference between these connection was or didn't notice one of these possibilities.

A similar problem conterns the level of abstractness of the links. When a room is created (which is always in bubble mode), the user might have some rought ideas regarding its door connections to other rooms. When a concret wall layout is entered, the existing connections kept. If a user wants to refine a certain connection (i.e. exchanging it by another connection that goes through a door or passage in the concrete wall layout), he is forced to manually delete the existing connection and to create a new one. Similarly, all connections through concrete doors or passages are deletect, when a new wall layout is entered. Both behaviours are rather unintuitive. Fortunately, these problems didn't appeared often during the user study. One way to overcome this problem more elegantly, is to employ a mechanism that suppresses the display the more abstract connection in the presence of a more concrete one (i.e. a door connection between a pair of two rooms is not displayed, if a door connections exists that connects doors in the concrete wall layout of the rooms). Likewise, a more advanced mechanism that allows to edit wall layouts instead of replacing them by new layouts could help to mitigate the mentioned problems.

Basically, most of the participants were capable of entering reasonable drawings using our prototypes. After some training, the participants were able to make use of the most functions of the interface and spend reasonable time on

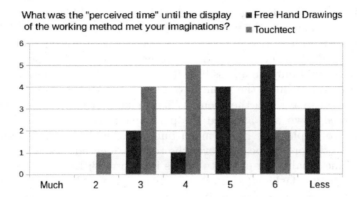

(a) Comparison of Perceived Time until Display meets imagination for free hand drawings and touchtect

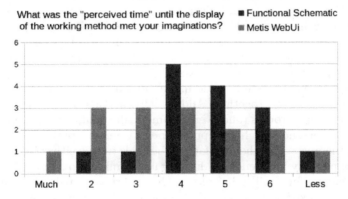

(b) Comparison of Perceived Time until Display meets imagination for Functional Diagrams and Metis WebUI

Fig. 10. The perceived time is both a measurement for the user's satisfaction and the efficiency.

handling them. TouchTect with its gestures appeared to be more easy and intuitive to use than the Metis WebUI, especially when it comes to drawing room shapes and linking the rooms. The biggest problem in the context of the Metis WebUI was that most participants did not make fully use of the possibility to connect the rooms as intended but led the rooms unconnected and focused on aligning the rooms manually to each other.

Apart from some rather minor cosmetic and usability flaws that attracted our attention during the study (e.g. some user confused the bubble mode with circle-shaped rooms), looking at the way how architects used the Metis WebUI helped us to find some points for design decisions we were not totally sure of before. For example we decided in the examined prototype that the radial menus of doors and windows should only be accessible after pressing the corresponding button in the main radial menu of the room in order to reduce the amount of buttons simultaneously displayed on the room. When looking at the videos we realized that this slowed down and annoyed the participants tremendously. Therefore, we are going to display the radial menu buttons of windows and doors in the next version of the prototype whenever the room is focused. Likewise, the resizing/scaling functionality for concrete rooms is unformed: Every room alone can be resized in stepless fashion (which is quite reasonable in the bubble mode), but room shapes can only be edited using a fixed grid (we wanted to avoid free-style drawings in the Metis WebUI). Hence, rooms can be resized so that their room length does not fit any longer the ones of other rooms. In the next version of the Metis WebUI we want to tackle this problem by a new resizing function that snaps when the wall corners of a room matches the size of a nearby room. Likewise, we want to incorporate a general snapping function for room movements. Snapped walls may be considered to be automatically connected by links which would speed up the drafting process and would appear more natural to the user. We also want to incorporate a "glue mode" in which rooms that are snapped are automatically moved together. Additionally, a function that automatically links walls of snapped rooms (and even automatically creates missing doors when rooms snap) is planned for future prototypes. A general problem arises, when considering the purpose of the interfaces: The tools can be either considered as a general (and possibly independent) drawing and thinking tool or as the interface to a search engine for similar floorplans. These purposes might diverge as illustrated with the link-drawing issue: The connecting lines have a certain meaning for a later-attached search mechanism. If these lines have another meaning in the mental model of the user (or the user isn't even aware of their existence), the user might think he/she expressed his/her thoughts correctly, but will get incongruous search result. The users should be aware these semantics when the tools are considered as a search interface. Hence, we considered the interfaces as drawing and thinking tools when asking the participants to what degree the display matched their imaginations. We consider a "explose" and "implode" functionality that move away the rooms from each other to that the floorplan looks like an exploded assembly drawing in a technical user manual and the user can see all existing connections. The implode function could then used to revert the explosion and even snaps rooms that were not snaped before by the user but connected by links. Also a function for coping rooms was desired by some users.

Apart of the evaluated free hand drawings and the modeling of spatial schemata, other paradigms like floor plan representations and zoning of shapes will be examined in the future. Moreover multimodal interaction strategies are necessary to let the architect freely use different abstractions of his/her design idea without interrupting the design process and lost of data. An additional user study involving a test of the prototypes including the search functionality is also thinkable.

The discussed prototype Metis WebUI as well as the TouchTect application are going to be combined with the retrieval system MetisCBR (and other retrieval systems) during the further Metis project development. The system uses the case-based reasoning (CBR) technique to retrieve the most similar semantic fingerprints to a given sketch from a case base (a special sort of a database). It is also based on the multi agent retrieval paradigm, where each retrieval agents task is to use the given similarity functions to retrieve the most similar fingerprint parts (such as rooms or their outer connections). The retrieval process will be controlled by a coordinator agent that is able to act as a case- and/or rule-based reasoner to find the best strategy for a particular user query. Hence, subsequent user studies that also take the user's reaction on the retrieved search results into account have to be conducted.

7 Conclusion

In this paper, we introduced two concepts for graphical user interfaces that could help to migrate state-of-the-art pen and paper working methods in early architectural design phases towards computer-based workings methods. We described the state of the art working methods as they take place in architecture generally and motivated the new approach. Then we described the two graphical user interfaces that we designed in detail. After that we presented the setup of a user study to prove the viability of the interfaces. Later we outlined the results of the user study we conducted according to the presented setup. Finally, we listed improvements we made based on the findings of the user study. Having two viable concepts for user interactions, further research regarding search concepts for similar floor plans will be carried out so that automated assistance for early conceptual design phases in architecture can be provided in future.

References

1. Buxton, W.: Sketching User Experience: Getting the Design Right and the Right Design. M. Kaufmann, San Francisco (2007)
2. Gänshirt, C.: Werkzeuge fr Ideen: Einfhrung ins architektonische Entwerfen. Birkhäuser, Basel (2007)
3. Hillier, B.: Space is the maschine (2007)
4. Langenhan, C., Weber, M., Liwicki, M., Petzold, F., Dengel, A.: Graph-based retrieval of building information models for supporting the early design stages. Adv. Eng. Inf. **27**(4), 413–426 (2013)

Recognizing Electronic Circuits to Enrich Web Documents for Electronic Simulation

Shubham Agarwal[✉], Mohit Agrawal[✉], and Santanu Chaudhury[✉]

Indian Institute of Technology Delhi, New Delhi, India
shubhamagarwal003@gmail.com, mohitleoagrawal@gmail.com,
santanuc@ee.iitd.ernet.in

Abstract. With the objective of creating an interface for experimenting with electronic circuits embedded in documents or images, in this paper we have presented a system for parsing and understanding of electronic circuit diagrams. The developed system consists of following steps- symbol extraction, symbol recognition, optimization and netlist-representation. Firstly, symbols are extracted from the image by removing text and connection lines using computer vision techniques. For symbol recognizer a probabilistic-SVM classifier is built using HOG and radon features on training data. A Bayesian framework is used to incorporate domain knowledge information to improve the performance of the probabilistic symbol recognizer. An novel optimization approach based on top-down features is used to remove the errors that occurs in the symbol extraction and recognition task. A depth first traversal algorithm is used to find the connections between the symbols and then image is represented in the form of usable data structure. The system is evaluated on a dataset of 20 analog electronic circuit images collected from various sources and the results are presented.

Keywords: Graphics recognition · Document image analysis · Bayesian inference · Domain knowledge · Top down optimization · Circuit netlist · Symbol recognition · Pattern recognition

1 Introduction

Schematic representations of electronic circuits are widely used to communicate know-how of electronic systems. However, computers need the representation in interpretable format for further analysis. There are many platform (like SPICE, VHDL Simulators, etc.) available which allows an user to represent circuits for both analysis and simulation. Many books, research papers, web documents, etc. contains circuits in the form of images. Given the abundance of circuit diagrams on the web, there is a need of an automatic tool which can be used to parse these images. Hence we propose a system that takes as input an electronic circuit image and returns a netlist like format and represent it in an interactive environment which provides functions like editing, simulating of circuits. This kind of system has various advantages. It could be used to enhance the learning experience by

© Springer International Publishing AG 2017
B. Lamiroy and R. Dueire Lins (Eds.): GREC 2015, LNCS 9657, pp. 60–74, 2017.
DOI: 10.1007/978-3-319-52159-6_5

making passive circuit images in the web documents an interactive entity with which experiments can be conducted.

A model to understand electronic circuit diagrams consists of extracting the symbols by separating characters and connection lines, recognizing those symbols and determining the connections between these symbols. A lot of research have been previously done on each individual task [5,9,20] but there are not much recent work which involves combining these tasks and build a complete system for circuit recognition. Specifically, [7] deals with electronic circuit diagrams but computationally intensive and does not aim circuit graphics typically present in web document or research papers. It also does not utilise domain information. An older approach [8] uses simple hand written heuristic for symbol recognizer and hard to scale. In recent years a lot of focus is on understanding of sketched diagrams on a similar kind of applications [1,2] and uses pen strokes features for symbol extraction, which are not available in images. Some older works [3] uses properties of connection lines to extract symbols but it require the image to be free of characters. The other work [4] proposes a system for recognizing digital circuit in which symbols mostly consists of loops. On the part of symbol recognition a lot of previous work are available. [5] combines various features in a Bayesian framework and present its results on GREC database [6]. In the context of electronic symbols [7] uses a convolution neural network, [8] uses rules purely based on domain specific knowledge. Our symbol recognizer uses both machine learning technique and incorporate domain knowledge rules in a Bayesian framework to improve the accuracy of recognizer. One of the novel contribution of our system is incorporating domain knowledge for top-down optimization as a feedback for increasing the overall accuracy of the system.

In Sect. 2, a overview of the system is provided. The four Sects. 3–6 discusses the main parts of the system individually. Finally, the effectiveness of the system is shown by results in Sect. 7.

2   Proposed Scheme

An electronic circuit image contains three types of components, i.e.; connection lines, symbols (like resistors, transistors, etc.) and text or characters which describes the properties (values) of the symbols. The system of understanding electronic circuit images can be broadly divided in the following tasks.

1. Symbol Extraction. This includes separating the text and connection lines from the image and identifying the location of symbols.
2. Recognizing the symbols that are being localized above.
3. Finding the connections between the symbols and finally representing it in a digital format.

Hence we propose a scheme that performs these basic tasks. Figure 1 presents the block diagram of our model. We used a bottom-up (+top-down) approach to remove the errors like failure to remove connection lines, or unnecessary categorizing a part of symbol as connection line, etc. which might occur in a strict bottom-up approach. The subsequent sections explains each tasks in detail.

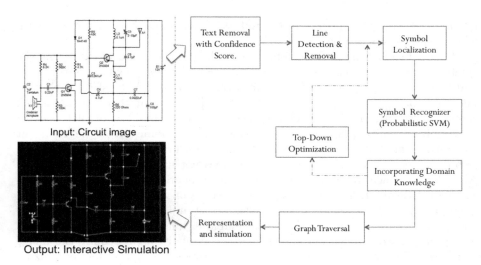

Fig. 1. Overview of our model for Parsing Electronic Circuits

3 Symbol Extraction

Individual symbols play an important role in parsing electronic circuits. Hence in our model the first task is the extraction of useful symbols from all kinds of components (text, connection lines, and symbols) in an image. Extraction of symbols contains three broad steps namely removal of text or characters, removal of connection lines and symbol localization.

3.1 Removal of Characters

Circuit images contains characters which are used to describe the properties of electronic symbols (like value of resistor, etc.) or can be of no significance. Further the characters decreases the accuracy of symbol recognizer as it act as a noise. Hence it is necessary to identify these characters and remove them from image. They could be later identified using an OCR and could be associated with the neighbouring symbol.

A system to separates text and graphics in an architectural floor plans is presented in [9]. It is based on the properties of connected components. Using the similar ideas and the fact that in any circuit image (or other line diagrams like pneumatic or hydraulic circuits) characters are part of connected components much smaller in size as compared to other symbols which are connected with each other and hence forms a larger connected component. To exploit this property a 2 dimensional feature vector corresponding to size (length and breadth) of the bounding box of the connected component was created for all the components of an image. K-Means clustering algorithm was then used to cluster these components in three clusters one belonging to characters and other two belonging to symbols (smaller in size compared to characters and larger in size compared to characters). Using just the clustering approach, there might be some confusion between characters and symbols. Figure 2 shows some instances in which such confusion might occur.

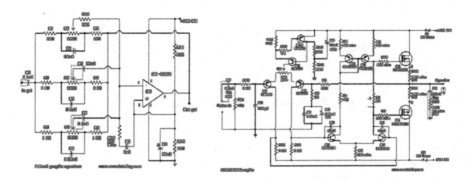

Fig. 2. Confusion between characters (in red) and symbols (in blue) in an image. (Color figure online)

Hence to avoid this confusion we used the fact that majority of connected components in the character cluster contains character and to remove mistaken points, following properties were considered for filtering. These are

1. Whether they contain any connection line.
2. Whether any extended connection line intersect the bounding box.

Since in any circuit (or line diagram) image these are some of the properties which could be used to distinguish characters and subsequently improve the character removal accuracy. After removing characters the modified image was considered for subsequent step of removing connection lines and symbol localization.

Figure 3 shows instances of character removal. The red squares corresponds to components which are considered as characters and green square corresponds to the components with low confidence score which doesn't follow the properties and hence were not considered as characters.

3.2   Connection Lines Detection and Removal

Once characters are removed schematics contains two types of components connection lines and symbols. Hence to extract the symbols it was necessary to remove connection lines. For detecting the connection lines we used various generic properties [3] that the connection lines of electronic circuit follows. Our input is computer aided electronic diagram and thus these properties would follow. Some of these properties are

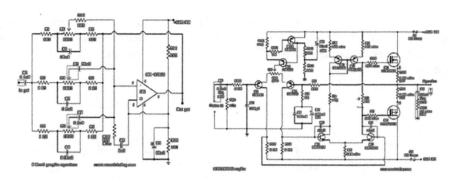

Fig. 3. Characters identified in an image.

1. Connection lines are mostly horizontal and vertical lines
2. Connection lines are not open lines i.e. they have a component at their end.
3. Simple loops belongs to the category of symbols.

Hence we used a Line Segment Detector (LSD) by R.G. von Gioi et al. [10] to detect all lines in an image. LSD is a state-of-the-art linear time algorithm to detect locally straight contours (lines) in an image with false detection control for noise. Once the line segments are detected, those line segments which satisfy the above properties were found. These line segments were considered to be connection lines and were removed from the image by replacing the pixels corresponding to the line segment with background pixels of the image. After removing the connection line what we obtain is a shredded image. Figure 4 shows a shredded image after removing the connection lines.

It may be possible that sometimes all the connection lines are not removed and two or more symbols are localized as one symbol or a line belonging to symbol is removed and hence the symbol is split in two or more pieces hence in our top-down optimization we take care of such problems that may occur in strictly bottom-up approach.

3.3   Symbol Localization

After removing the connection lines from an image, a shredded image is obtained. To localize symbols a connected component analysis was done on the shredded image and bounding boxes were obtained about the different components. The overlapping boxes were merged in one big box corresponding to the envelope of both the boxes. After obtaining the bounding box the corresponding region of the image was considered to be potential symbols. Figure 5 shows an example of application of the process on a sample image.

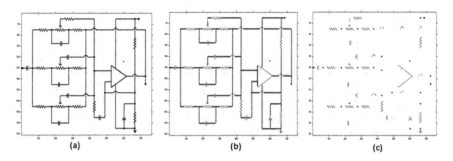

Fig. 4. Removal of connection lines. (a) Image after Character Removal. (b) Lines Detected. (c) Shredded Image after removal of connection lines

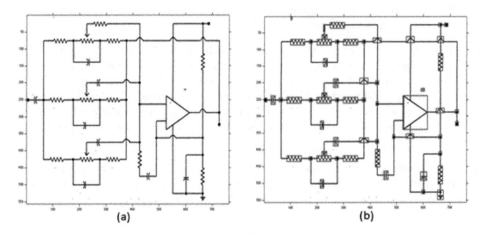

Fig. 5. Connected component analysis. (a) Image after Character Removal. (b) Bounding box detected around the potential symbols

4 Symbol Recognition-Probabilistic SVM and Domain Knowledge Update

After extracting the symbols the other major task is recognizing these symbols. The state-of-art [11] on a similar kind of problem of digit recognizer uses convolution neural network (CNN). The major drawback of the CNN is that for larger networks it leads to over-fitting on a smaller dataset. The GREC 2011 dataset TC10 [23] of about 250 symbols is limited to only a few varieties and the dataset collected by us was limited, hence we used a symbol recognizer based on probabilistic SVM. The performance of classifier is improved by incorporating domain knowledge in a Bayesian framework. The input to symbol recognizer is a fixed size (50×50) image and output is a probability distribution over the classes of symbols.

4.1   Dataset

For collecting the dataset for building a symbol recognizer we scrapped circuit images from various resources like Google images, CircuitLabs.com [12], and other hobby sites and extracted symbols from these images. We then manually label these symbols into 9 classes i.e.; capacitor, diode, ground, inductor, junction, opamp, transistor, resistor and none (other than above classes). A total of 3847 symbol images were collected. These images were then randomly divided into a training (70% of total) and test (30% of total) set.

4.2   Features

For the classifying an image, each symbol image was scaled to a constant size of 50×50 with centre of the original image coinciding with the centre of the scaled image. The features used were

1. HOG - Histogram of Oriented Gradient [13] are the features that count the gradient orientation in localized region of an image. The HOG features were selected as the local shape of an object is captured by its gradient.
2. R-Signature - R-Signature [14] are the features which uses Radon Transform. These are the marginalized Radon Transform along the intensity. The R-Sign features were selected as they corresponds to the orientation of lines in an image.

The dimension of feature vector obtained was $4356\,(\text{HOG}) + 181$ (R-Signature) $= 4537$. These features were then normalized and projected to a lower dimension of 100 using Principal Component Analysis.

4.3   Classification-Probabilistic SVM

The classifier used for classification was a multi-class (one-vs-one) SVM which gives probability estimates of the different classes. Inherently SVM predicts only the class and doesn't give any probability estimates for the classes. Wu et al. [15] proposes various methods which could be used to extend SVM and estimate the probabilities over different classes. We used the second approach suggested by Wu et al. [15] and implemented in libsvm [16]. We used RBF kernel for the SVM. The parameters Cost (C) and γ were estimated with standard grid-search method.

4.4   Domain Knowledge Incorporation

After having applied a Probabilistic-SVM, we obtain a probability mass function over the available classes. For incorporating the domain knowledge information, we adopted a conditional probability model. The domain knowledge information about the symbols has to be learnt a priori. Since in electronic circuits each symbols have specific number of connections and further the symmetry of connection lines (lines entering and leaving must be symmetric w.r.t symbols) are also followed, hence we used the number of connections and the symmetry of connections as features for domain knowledge update. Number of connections is taken by counting number of connection from outside the symbol area while symmetry of connection is a 4-dimensional variable corresponding to mean location of lines entering from all the 4 sides. These both features are discretized into finite discrete bins. The Eq. 1 is used to find the posterior probability over the symbol classes. For a test symbol, Probabilistic-SVM provides the prior i.e. P(S) and $P(C|S)\&P(Symm|S)$ are learnt from the training data. Smoothing was also used in the learning to allow non-zero probability for non-frequent feature values.

$$P(S|C, Symm) = \frac{P(C, Symm|S) * P(S)}{P(C, Symm)}$$
$$= \frac{P(C|S)P(Symm|S)P(S)}{P(C, Symm)}$$

(1)

where,
S-Class of Symbol
C-No. of Connection
Symm-Symmetry of Connection Lines

4.5   Performance of Symbol Recognition

To test the performance of our symbol recognizer, we trained the probabilistic SVM and the domain knowledge model using the training set as was described in Sect. 4.1. The recognizer was tested on the test set by both without incorporating domain knowledge and incorporating domain knowledge. The accuracy obtained was 93% (without incorporating domain knowledge) and 95% (with incorporating domain knowledge).

5   Top down Optimization

The symbol recognizer outputs rectangle co-ordinates with symbol label attached to document. At the end of the symbol recognizer's output, the possible problems (shown in Fig. 6) up to this step are the following:

1. Two or more symbols might have merged together.
2. A symbol might have broken into two or more parts.
3. Some symbols might have misclassified due to either erroneous classifier or improper symbol input.

The majority of errors occurs as the 3rd problem occurring due to first two. In absence of any further refinements, the parsing is completely based on the bottom-up features used in the symbol recognizer i.e. HOG, radon in the Probabilistic-SVM and lines information in the Bayesian update.

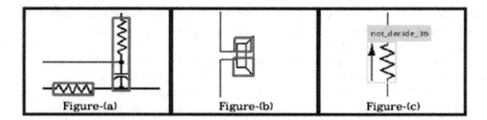

Fig. 6. Wrong symbol extraction (a) due to merging of two adjacent symbols (b) due to splitting of a symbol (c) and subsequent misclassification

A well known sentence parsing problem, syntactic analysis, is dealt in language science. In this field, approaches ranging from strictly bottom up to a combination of bottom-up and top-down are well studied [17]. In speech recognition, a logogen model [18] suggests usage of top-down features to aid the bottom-up features for improved inference. Inspired from this idea, we use a similar approach to improve the circuit recognition rates by incorporating the top-down domain level features.

We have introduced a score that measures the validity of the circuit parse and then obtained the optimum circuit parse by maximising that score. The maximisation step took into account the inter-symbol features like neighbourhood, connections and used them to improve the score. This is done iteratively to maximize the validity of circuit at each step. We propose that operation we perform are able to deal with all of the occurred problems when they are segregated as per aforementioned categories. The problems that might The next section will cover the score formulation, the operations that can improve the score and then the algorithm to enable the score maximisation using the operations.

5.1   Symbol Confidence Score

The symbols predicted from the recognizer might be inconsistent with their domain information; e.g. connectivity of the symbol with adjoining circuit. Also, a low probability over the symbol category implies less confidence hence high chances of error. Thus to measure the confidence of a symbol over its predicted category, we incorporated these factors as given below.

$$Symbol\ Confidence\ Score = \alpha * \beta * \gamma \tag{2}$$

where,
α = Probability of predicted class, $\alpha \in [0,1]$
β = Confidence on the number of connection according to the predicted class, $\beta \in \{0.1,1\}$
γ = Confidence on symmetry of connections, $\gamma \in [0,1]$

In the above equation, β is a binary variable to indicate whether number of connection of the symbol are consistent with the domain knowledge and it can take values 1 and 0.1. γ is variable to indicate how symmetrically are the connection lines placed around the symbol. As per the general schematics convention and symbols [19], all the symbols have symmetry with respect to connection lines joining them i.e. centroid of points where connection lines enters the symbol box from left side aligns horizontally with the centroid of points where connection lines enters the symbol box from right side. Same condition holds for vertical connection lines. Any difference in alignment reduces the confidence score γ linearly and thus symbol confidence score can take values from 0 to 1. So a higher symbol confidence score (close to 1) implies high values of α, β and γ which is true for a correct prediction. Thus, we can utilise this score to improve upon the prediction which will be done with the help of operations defined in the next section.

5.2   Basic Operations

To rectify the problem of symbol merging and getting split in multiple parts, following operations on the symbol were designed using image processing techniques.

SPLIT and LOCALISE Operation. These operations can resolve problem when the rectangle labelled as symbol in symbol recognition step contains anything more than one symbol. In a scenario similar to image in left side of Fig. 7, the symbol extraction resulted in an erroneous symbol. This needs to broken down into two separate components. We used the Radon transform [21] to identify the possible horizontal or vertical lines that can break it. The magnitude of radon transform is the line integral of the image along a particular line. We select only the horizontal and vertical lines corresponding to points having magnitude of radon transform below a certain threshold. Out the these lines, thickest lines which can break the image into two are taken. If no such lines are found at a threshold, the threshold is increased to allow more lines to break the image. If an upper limit on threshold is reached, we return the original image with the peripherals omitted. So in the absence of any blue lines as shown in Fig. 8, it would have resulted in localised image tearing off the boundary part of the image.

MERGE Operation. This operation can resolve problem when rectangle labelled as a symbol in symbol recognition step do not contains less than one full symbol and the complementary part is also present in any of the other detected symbols. When two neighbouring parts are identified to be belonging to the same symbol, they are directly joined to form a bigger symbol with an inclusion of the intermediate portions of the image. This operation results in rectangle which circumscribe the rectangles of the two part.

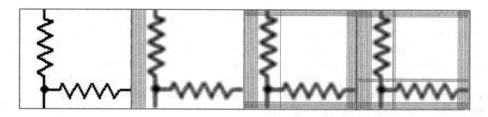

Fig. 7. SPLIT Operation on (a) Original Image while the blue lines indicates the horizontal and vertical lines whose radon transform is below a (b) threshold = 0.5 (c) threshold = 1.5 (d) threshold = 2.1; The image is then split from the blue lines that can break the image (Color figure online)

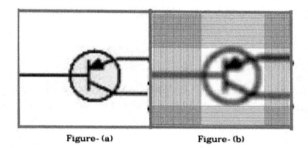

Figure- (a)   Figure- (b)

Fig. 8. LOCALISE Operation on (a) Original Image (b) In absence of split lines, Image is localised

5.3   Algorithm for the Optimization

The general idea of the optimization is to maximise the symbol confidence score defined in Eq. 2 for all the symbols through out the image. This will done with allowing the SPLIT, LOCALISE and MERGE operation on symbol images. Importantly, any of these operations are performed if and only if the resulting configuration is better in terms of Symbol Confidence score. Algorithm begins dealing with lowest scored symbols and they are due to aforementioned three reasons. The symbols that are broken into many pieces will have constituents as low score symbols. So if such pair of symbols occurs in horizontal and vertical neighbourhood, they have high chances of forming an meaningful symbol by combining them. So first MERGE operation is tried on such cases. And in the absence of such pairs, the erroneous symbol might have be to be broken in parts and this is done using SPLIT or LOCALISE. These iterations are performed until all there are no unchecked low score symbols. Some of the steps of configuration changes in an example image are shown in the images given in Fig. 9.

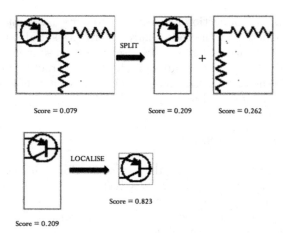

Fig. 9. Algorithm on part of Original Image and the operations performed

6   Connection Between Components

Once the symbols were localized and recognized and the top-down approach were incorporated, it is finally required to find the connection relation between various components to represent in digitally. Hence to find the connection relation, a Depth First Search based algorithm was used. In this case each dark pixel of the image is considered as node and edges exists between adjacent nodes if and only if both are dark.

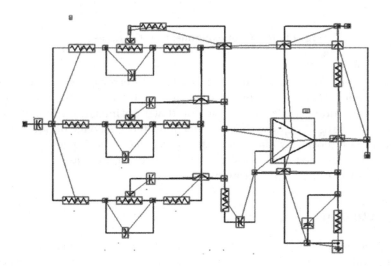

Fig. 10. Connection detected in a circuit

Figure 10 shows the connection between components in a sample image. Once the connections are detected, the code finally generates a suitable file which could be passed to an open source simulator. We used the open source simulator "Java Circuit Simulator" [22]. This simulator provides an interactive method to edit, simulate, plot current or voltage, etc. in a circuit. A snapshot of a simulated circuit is present in output of Fig. 1.

7   Results and Discussion

To evaluate our model we selected a dataset of 20 circuit images from various resources like Google Images, CircuitLabs [12], etc., parsed them and found various statistics. The statistics were selected so as to represent the performance of each task i.e., symbol extraction and symbol recognition. We have taken the following statistics to measure the performance of model.

1. Symbol extraction error i.e. number of symbols missed in a circuit schematic,
2. Recognition error i.e. system fails to determine the correct class of the symbol
3. Low confidence symbols i.e. symbols which are classified with low probability

The results are presented in Fig. 11. Majority of the Recognition error and Low confidence symbols were due to symbols not included in the training data like Loudspeaker, not-connected crossing, etc.

No. of Images	No. of symbols	Extraction Error	Recognition Error	Low Confidence
20	952	6.3%	5.28%	9.66%

Fig. 11. Result of experiment on the dataset

In the model, top-down optimization resolves the error in recognition of symbols but cannot if the error is outside the symbols. If the recall of symbol detection is high, accuracy is dependent on top-down optimization. Our system is also robust towards images with noisy unconnected elements because most of such items are removed by classifying them into characters. Line detection and removal is also designed to be robust towards noise [10] but case of deteriorated images needs to be handled separately.

8   Conclusion

A system to automatically understand the electronic circuit images was developed and evaluated. Such a system can semanticize vast plethora of electronic circuit images present on research papers, hobby community sites and general articles. The methodology developed makes use of domain knowledge information separately. A modular approach to enhance the quality of inference is proposed in the top-down optimization. Thus, this approach can be used in other categories of engineering drawing with similar structure of symbols and connections. Also, confidence score developed using the probabilistic framework enables us to identify misclassification beforehand. In practice, this system also provides opportunity to include user feedback to report new symbols or representation with minimal editing. So the system can itself learn and improve even for unaccounted symbols. We consider formalization of the domain information as one of the future extension.

References

1. LaViola Jr., J.J., Zeleznik, R.C.: MathPad 2: a system for the creation and exploration of mathematical sketches. In: ACM SIGGRAPH 2007 Courses. ACM (2007)
2. Murugappan, S., Ramani, K.: Feasy: a sketch-based interface integrating structural analysis in early design. In: ASME 2009 International Design Engineering Technical Conferences and Computers and Information in Engineering Conference. American Society of Mechanical Engineers (2009)
3. Yu, Y., Samal, A., Seth, S.: Isolating symbols from connection lines in a class of engineering drawings. Pattern Recogn. **27**(3), 391–404 (1994)
4. Okazaki, A., et al.: An automatic circuit diagram reader with loop-structure-based symbol recognition. IEEE Trans. Pattern Anal. Mach. Intell. **10**(3), 331–341 (1988)
5. Barrat, S., Tabbone, S., Nourrissier, P.: A bayesian classifier for symbol recognition. In: Seventh International Workshop on Graphics Recognition, GREC 2007 (2007)
6. Lladós, J., Kwon, Y.-B. (eds.): GREC 2003. LNCS, vol. 3088. Springer, Heidelberg (2004)
7. Fu, L., Kara, L.B.: From engineering diagrams to engineering models: visual recognition and applications. Comput. Aided Des. **43**(3), 278–292 (2011)
8. Yu, Y., Samal, A., Seth, S.C.: A system for recognizing a large class of engineering drawings. IEEE Trans. Pattern Anal. Mach. Intell. **19**(8), 868–890 (1997)
9. Ahmed, S., et al.: Text/graphics segmentation in architectural floor plans. In: 2011 International Conference on Document Analysis and Recognition (ICDAR). IEEE (2011)
10. Von Gioi, R.G., et al.: LSD: a line segment detector. Image Process. On Line **2**(3), 35–55 (2012)
11. Ciresan, D., Meier, U., Schmidhuber, J.: Multi-column deep neural networks for image classification. In: 2012 IEEE Conference on Computer Vision and Pattern Recognition (CVPR). IEEE (2012)
12. CircuitLab - online schematic editor and circuit simulator, February 2015. https://www.circuitlab.com/
13. Dalal, N., Triggs, B.: Histograms of oriented gradients for human detection. In: IEEE Computer Society Conference on Computer Vision and Pattern Recognition. CVPR 2005, vol. 1. IEEE (2005)
14. Tabbone, S., Wendling, L.: Technical symbols recognition using the two-dimensional radon transform. In: 2002 Proceedings of 16th International Conference on Pattern Recognition, vol. 3. IEEE (2002)
15. Wu, T.-F., Lin, C.-J., Weng, R.C.: Probability estimates for multi-class classification by pairwise coupling. J. Mach. Learn. Res. **5**, 975–1005 (2004)

16. Chang, C.-C., Lin, C.-J.: LIBSVM: a library for support vector machines. ACM Trans. Intel. Syst. Technol. (TIST) **2**(3), 27:1–27:27 (2011)
17. Rosenfield, R.: Two decades of statistical language modeling: where do we go from here? (2000)
18. Morton, J.: The logogen model and orthographic structure. In: Cognitive Processes in Spelling, pp. 117–133 (1980)
19. Typical Electrical Drawing Symbols and Conventions. Accessed 3 July 2015. http://pbadupws.nrc.gov/docs/ML1025/ML102530301.pdf
20. Lladós, J., Valveny, E., Sánchez, G., Martí, E.: Symbol recognition: current advances and perspectives. In: Blostein, D., Kwon, Y.-B. (eds.) GREC 2001. LNCS, vol. 2390, pp. 104–128. Springer, Heidelberg (2002). doi:10.1007/3-540-45868-9_9
21. Tabbone, S., Wendling, L., Salmon, J.-P.: A new shape descriptor defined on the radon transform. Comput. Vis. Image Underst. **102**(1), 42–51 (2006)
22. Falstad, P.: Circuit Simulator Applet. Accessed 25 April 2015. http://www.falstad.com/circuit/
23. Valveny, E., Delalandre, M., Raveaux, R., Lamiroy, B.: Report on the symbol recognition and spotting contest. In: Kwon, Y.-B., Ogier, J.-M. (eds.) GREC 2011. LNCS, vol. 7423, pp. 198–207. Springer, Heidelberg (2013). doi:10.1007/978-3-642-36824-0_19

Ontology-Based Understanding
of Architectural Drawings

Lluís-Pere de las Heras, Oriol Ramos Terrades[✉], and Josep Lladós

Computer Vision Center, Universitat Autònoma de Barcelona,
Campus UAB, 08193 Bellatera, Barcelona, Catalonia, Spain
{lpheras,oramos,josep}@cvc.uab.es
http://www.cvc.uab.cat

Abstract. In this paper we present a knowledge base of architectural documents aiming at improving existing methods of floor plan classification and understanding. It consists of an ontological definition of the domain and the inclusion of real instances coming from both, automatically interpreted and manually labeled documents. The knowledge base has proven to be an effective tool to structure our knowledge and to easily maintain and upgrade it. Moreover, it is an appropriate means to automatically check the consistency of relational data and a convenient complement of hard-coded knowledge interpretation systems.

Keywords: Graphics recognition · Floor plan analysis · Domain ontology

1 Introduction

Graphical documents convey complex semantic concepts understandable by humans. This information is structured agreeing to a visual language; consisting of a vocabulary –graphical symbols– and a syntax –contextual relations–. Therefore, the semantic content expressed in a document is defined by the contextualized meaning of its structurally related symbols. Let us exemplify this fact by making an analogy to natural languages. The following two sentences are correct in terms of vocabulary and syntax:

People drive cars

Cars drive people

Even though both sentences consist of the same set of words, their structure –syntactical positioning– leads them to express completely different meanings. Moreover, given our natural knowledge of the language domain –the real world–, we can assert that one of the sentences expresses an unlikely event.

Alike to natural language comprehension, graphical document understanding requires the knowledge of the document domain. This knowledge defines the meaning of the compounding items in a determined context. For instance, the color, the shape, and the relative location of objects in a document agree to a defined visual knowledge in order to express desirable semantic concepts.

© Springer International Publishing AG 2017
B. Lamiroy and R. Dueire Lins (Eds.): GREC 2015, LNCS 9657, pp. 75–85, 2017.
DOI: 10.1007/978-3-319-52159-6_6

Therefore, to make computers able to understand graphical documents, we need to provide them with the appropriate tools to define, store, and employ this knowledge.

Ontologies are machine-interpretable specifications of conceptualizations [9]. They make explicit the description of concepts (classes), their attributes (properties), and mutual relationships that can exist in a domain. The domain definitions are written in formal languages with an expressive power close to the first-order logic; the language definition is independent to the data structure. Therefore, ontologies allow to describe a domain knowledge in a manner that it can be reused, incremented, and shared by disparate agents. Additionally, an ontological definition together with individual instances of the classes conforms a knowledge base that can be analyzed, queried, and classified semantically. Ontological definitions have already demonstrated their suitability in multiple Computer Vision scenarios, e.g. object categorization [14] and recognition [19], medical imaging [15], and natural image description [16]. Additionally, strongly related to our framework, Bhatt et al. present in [5] an ontological formalization of the architectural design domain that tries to link the earlier structural perception of an architect with the actual functionality of a design. In consequence, and given their properties, ontologies are convenient tools to express the domain of graphical documents.

In this paper we present a tentative exploration of the ontological modeling for graphical document understanding. More specifically, we have created a domain ontology of architectural drawings that allows us to perform semantic classification, retrieval, and validation of these documents. In Sect. 2, we introduce the floor plan knowledge base. Section 3 is devoted to overview the experiments performed. Finally, in Sect. 4 we conclude this paper.

2   Floor Plan Knowledge Base

We have created a knowledge base consisting of a formal definition of floor plan documents and a set real instances coming from both, automatic interpretation and manual annotation. This knowledge base has been created with the aim of filling the following intentions:

- To define specifically the semantics of our domain. We have created a floor plan ontology that permits us to describe formally the taxonomy of the concepts conveyed in floor plans, their properties, and relations.
- To permit the reutilization and maintenance of the domain. Since this is a long term project, the formal definition of the domain eases its maintenance; there is an independence between the interacting implementations and the ontology. Moreover, it allows to other agents, either human or automatic, to reuse and upgrade our definition at their convenience.
- To allow semantic reasoning with real data. The inclusion of instances agreeing the ontological framework allow to classify and validate them regarding the definition of the concepts, attributes, and relations.

The knowledge base is defined using the Web Ontology Language OWL2 [11] on the Protégé5 [3] ontology editor. In the following we summarize the reasons of these decisions.

- OWL2 is a logic-based description language for the semantic web that is able to explicitly represent complex knowledge about things and their relations. The expressiveness of OWL2 to represent machine-interpretable content overcomes other existing languages such as RDF [4], DAML [17], and DAML+OIL [6]. Several semantic reasoners exist for OWL, as Fact++ from the University of Manchester and Hermit from the University of Oxford, which allow inferring automatically semantic properties of ontology defined-classes. Furthermore, the Semantic Web Rule Language SWRL [12] is an extension of the OWL model-theoretic semantics that provides a formal meaning to OWL ontologies by including Horn-like rules written in RuleML. By this means, instance-based semantic assumptions in floor plan classes can be added to our ontology and automatically be reasoned. Finally, query languages as SPARQL [10] and OWL-SAIQL [13] allow to query the OWL ontology similarly to SQL for relational databases. OWL2, SWRL, and SPARQL are taken as W3C recommendation, which assures their promotion, maintenance, and upgrade.
- Protégé is a software developed by the University of Stanford to construct ontologies and knowledge-based applications in a friendly UI. It is currently used in several research and private projects given its wide spectrum of functionalities for ontology design and application.[1] It supports, among others, OWL, SWRL, and SPARQL.

In the following, we firstly explain the floor plan ontology and we subsequently describe how we have integrated real data into it.

2.1 Floor Plan Ontology

The design of the floor plan ontology started by deciding the functionality that it is intended to. In our case, we have constructed an ontology to represent the knowledge of floor plan documents within the scope of architectural understanding. This definition encapsulates the structural configuration of these documents, the classes (concepts), properties (attributes), and relations (contextual dependences). Despite it is worthy to remark that this is our own definition and it will vary for different applications, images, and experts, we have defined this ontology taking into account several considerations. We have contacted a team of architects to address their needs in automatic interpretation applications. We experienced several cooperations with research and private companies aiming for different applications related to floor plan interpretation. We have considered other floor plan definitions in the literature that entail some sort of structural understanding, such is the case of [21] for evacuation building simulation, and [20] for structural floor plan retrieval. Additionally, we have also been inspired

---

[1] http://protege.cim3.net/cgi-bin/wiki.pl?ProjectsThatUseProtege.

by the relevance of the structural information for high-level understanding in graphical documents, i.e. flowchart interpretation in patent documents [18].

Let us further describe the main elements of the ontology:

- **Class Taxonomy:** The classes in the ontology define objects or concepts. In our case, the classes are the structural concepts appearing in architectural drawings: Building, Room, Domain, Wall, Door, Window, etc. Notice that these classes are disjoint under a semantic point of view. This means that one instance can only belong to one of the defined classes, e.g a *wall* belonging to the class Wall cannot be at the same time an instance of the Room. Semantically, all these classes are disjoint siblings from a common parent class named StructuralElement, see Fig. 1. For instance, a building is a individual of the class Building, which is a *kind of* StructuralElement.

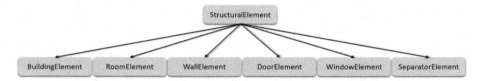

Fig. 1. Class taxonomy.

- **Object Properties:** Object properties are pairwise relations between individuals. In the floor plan ontology they describe the structural dependences that can relate two objects. For instance, rooms may be related in terms of *neighborhood* and *accessibility*, and walls, doors and windows in terms of *incidence*, see Fig. 2. Furthermore, we also define a taxonomy of object properties, e.g. the relations *hasRoom*, *hasWall*, *hasDoor*, *hasWindow*, and *hasSeparation* are subproberties of *hasStructuralElement*. This last relation is transitive, which implies that, when a individual *A hasStructuralElement B* and, at the same time, this *B hasStructuralElement C*, *A hasStructuralElement C*.
- **Data Properties:** The object classes may have defined some properties or attributes that link their individuals to an XML Schema Datatype. For instance, we defined in our syntactic representation that buildings and rooms cover an area or space in a building. Therefore, we define a data property named *hasArea* that relates the individuals of these classes with a numerical value. In Fig. 3 we show the data properties for the StucturalElements.

2.2   Introducing Real Instances into Our Knowledge Base

Once our domain is described, we have created a knowledge base by introducing real instances into the ontological definition. Our aim is to perform semantic reasoning on this data and thus, to validate our ontological design together with our incoming floor plan representations. This input data comes from two different sources. On the one hand, it is acquired from the floor plan interpretation

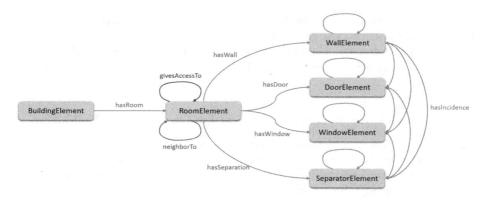

Fig. 2. Object properties.

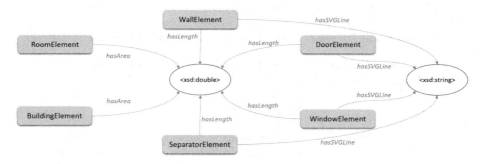

Fig. 3. Data properties.

method in [7]. This recognition approach outputs the graph representation that carries the structure of each document. On the other hand, it is collected from the structured groundtruth in [8]. These manually annotated documents not only incorporate the labellings of the objects, but they also make explicit the structural relations between objects.

Even though there are several frameworks and APIs available to transform our definition into a practicable implementations, e.g. Jena [1] and Sesame [2] in JAVA^{TM}, we have addressed this task in the opposite way. We have introduced our instances into the OWL definition and thus, used Protégé to perform the reasoning. This has been done by implementing a simple wrapper that is able to parse both, the interpreted representations and the SVG files from the groundtruth.

3   Experimental Validation

In this section we explain two use-cases for our knowledge-base of floor plans as examples of the multiple possibilities when semantic reasoning is available.

Firstly, we show how the automatic reasoning has helped us to perform further classification of our knowledge agreeing to new class definitions. Secondly, we show how this automatic classification has allowed us to do both, validate the consistency of our groundtruth and to improve a strictly bottom-up interpretation method.

3.1   Automatic Instance Classification for Groundtruth Validation

On the ontological specification presented in this paper, we have created new object classes whose individuals comply certain characteristics. Then, we use the reasoner to automatically compute the new class hierarchy and classify the instances that satisfy that specifications.

We have created a new object property namely *isPerimeterOf* that relates an architectural physical primitive –wall, door, or window– with a building instance; it specifies that a certain primitive is part of the exterior perimeter of a particular building. Then, we can define three object classes ExteriorWallElement, ExteriorDoorElement, and ExteriorWindowElement consisting of exterior primitives:

ExteriorWall := WallElement **and** (isPerimeterOf **some** BuildingElement)
ExteriorDoor := DoorElement **and** (isPerimeterOf **some** BuildingElement)
ExteriorWindow := WindowElement **and** (isPerimeterOf **some** BuildingElement).

When we run the reasoner, it automatically infers that ExteriorWall, ExteriorDoor, and ExteriorWindow are actually subclasses of WallElement, DoorElement, and WindowElement respectively. Furthermore, it automatically classifies that primitive individuals with a valid *isPerimeterOf* relation. Now we want to define what an exterior room is. We can do it as follows:

ExteriorRoom := RoomElement
and ((hasWall **some** ExteriorWall)
or (hasDoor **some** ExteriorDoor)
or (hasWindow **some** ExteriorWindow)).

Therefore, an exterior room is a room instance that has a wall, a door, or a window that belongs to the exterior perimeter of a building. Let's now define what an entrance room of a building is:

EntranceRoom := RoomElement
and (hasDoor some ExteriorDoor).

The reader may notice that both, ExteriorRoom and EntranceRoom are defined as subclasses of RoomElement. Yet, the reasoner actually infers that the class EntranceRoom is a subclass of ExteriorRoom, i.e. all instances of EntranceRoom are instances of ExteriorRoom at the same time. Figure 4 shows a snapshot of the class hierarchy before and after applying the reasoner. This feature is really helpful when the size of the ontology (the number of classes) starts to significantly increase and keeping the semantic consistency becomes a challenging task.

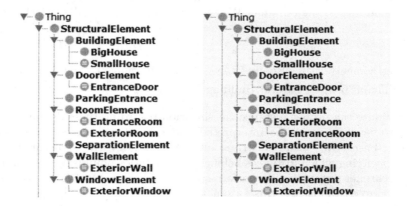

Fig. 4. Class hierarchy before and after the automatic inference.

Now, we can imagine that this knowledge base belongs to real estate company that allows to search online their available flats for rent. It may be interesting to classify the dwellings according to their usable space. Therefore, we can predefine some classes to define different building types concerning their area:

$$Studio := BuildingElement$$
$$\textbf{and } hasArea \textbf{ double}[<= 20]$$

$$SmallHouse := BuildingElement$$
$$(\textbf{and } hasArea \textbf{ double}[> 20])$$
$$(\textbf{and } hasArea \textbf{ double}[<= 70])$$

$$BigHouse := BuildingElement$$
$$\textbf{and } hasArea \textbf{ double}[> 70].$$

We can also declare this classes using SWRL. For instance in the case of the Studio:

BuildingElement($?x$), hasArea($?x, ?y$), lessThanOrEqual($?y, 20$) $\rightarrow$ Studio($?x$).

SWRL also allow us to define constrains between relationships. For instance, we can define that all the rooms that are accessible from each other are also neighbors:

$$givesAccessTo(?x, ?y) \rightarrow hasNeighbor(?x, ?y).$$

Finally, imagine that we are very interested on finding buildings that are exterior because we do like natural illumination at home. The semantic concept of exterior building can be defined as those building instances that at least have 3 rooms at the boundaries of the building. We therefore can define the ExteriorBuilding class as:

$$BuildingElement(?x), hasRoom(?x, ?y), ExteriorRoom(?y), makeBag(?b, ?y),$$
$$greaterThan(?b, 2) \rightarrow ExteriorBuilding(?x).$$

To validate the proper instance classification regarding these definitions, we have introduced some of the interpreted and groundtruth instances into our knowledge-base. Our wrapper writes into the ontology the structured data, already specifying which instances belong to the exterior boundary of a building, and the reasoner automatically performs the classification. In Fig. 5, we show a simple example to illustrate this automatic classification.

Individuals	Class	Inferred relations	Data properties
◆ Building1	● BuildingElement	▣ hasParentChildRelation Wall24	▣ hasArea 10.0
◆ Building104	● Studio	▣ hasParentChildRelation Wall25	
◆ Building13		▣ hasParentChildRelation Wall26	
◆ Building2		▣ hasParentChildRelation Wall27	
◆ Building23			
◆ Building32			
◆ Building50			
◆ Building84			

Fig. 5. Automatic instance classification. The reasoner categorizes the instance *Building104* as a Studio according to its area. The reasoner also infers the building *parentChildRelation* with those primitives that belong to its rooms.

3.2 Groundtruth Validation and Automatic Interpretation Improvement

The automatic verification of the instance description w.r.t the domain ontology has been a crucial process for the generation of the consistent floor plan groundtruth, named CVC-FP, presented in [8]. We have created a labeling tool[2] that allows to make specific the structural relations between the different architectural elements. Nevertheless, this tool does not control whether the relations between instances are well defined in terms of the knowledge model. Since the manual annotation is susceptible to errors, the consistency of labeled images can be strongly harmed. Therefore, we have incorporated every groundtruthed image into our knowledge base and have used the reasoner to spot transgressing

---

[2] The SGT-tool and the CVC-FP database are freely available at http://dag.cvc.uab.es/resources/floorplans.

instances w.r.t the domain definition. From the 122 labeled images, 23 labeling errors have been reported. Most of them produced by a violation of the structural relations domain or scope. For instance, when trying to define as accessible a wall and a room instances. In these cases, the reasoner outputs the encountered inconsistency and facilitates the correction of the mislabeled images.

In addition to that, we have used our domain definition to add a semantic layer on top of the bottom-up interpretation presented in [7]. This layer analyzes the graph representation output by the system and allows to detect inconsistencies w.r.t the knowledge model. For instance, the domain definition states that every room in a floor plan must be neighborly connected to at least another room. Therefore, the knowledge model can parse the room connectivity graph and discard those instances that are isolated. Quantitatively, this semantic analysis improves the recognition accuracy on two of the four datasets of the CVC-FP. These database is composed of real images split into datasets according to the graphical notation of the walls: Black, Textured, Textured2, and Parallel. On the Textured dataset from 85.7% to 89.4%, and in the Textured2 dataset from 40.4% to 41.7%. Meanwhile, the results on the Black and Parallel datasets remain the unaltered. This enhancement on both textured datasets is produced by the fact that, on these collections, multiple false positive rooms are obtained at the outskirts of the building models, see an example in Fig. 6, but they are detected and ruled out by semantic reasoner.

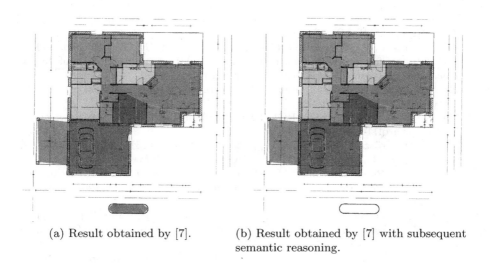

(a) Result obtained by [7].   (b) Result obtained by [7] with subsequent semantic reasoning.

Fig. 6. Semantic reasoning impact on room segmentation.

4   Conclusions

In this paper, we have created an ontological definition of the semantic meaning expressed in floor plan documents. This ontology has allowed us to specifically define the architectural concepts, their attributes, and relations. This ontology has been written in the Ontology Web Language due to its expressibility power and its multiple available tools. Furthermore, we have created a knowledge base of floor plans by introducing real instances of conveniently annotated documents into our semantic definition. This knowledge-base has allowed us to improve the performance of a recent floor plan interpretation system and to correct the manual mislabelings on a structural database of floor plans.

References

1. Apache Jena - A free and open source Java framework for building Semantic Web and Linked Data applications (2014). https://jena.apache.org/index.html
2. OpenRDF Sesame - A de-facto standard framework for processing RDF data (2014). http://www.openrdf.org
3. Protégé 5: A free, open-source ontology editor and framework for building intelligent systems (2014). http://protege.stanford.edu
4. RDF: Resource Description Framework (2014). http://www.w3.org/RDF/
5. Bhatt, M., Hois, J., Kutz, O.: Ontological modelling of form and function for architectural design. Appl. Ontol. **7**(3), 233–267 (2012)
6. Connolly, D., van Harmelen, F., Horrocks, I., McGuinness, D.L., Patel-Schneider, P.F., Stein, L.A.: DAML+OIL: Reference Description (2001). http://www.w3.org/TR/daml+oil-reference
7. de las Heras, L.-P., Ahmed, S., Liwicki, M., Valveny, E., Sánchez, G.: Statistical segmentation and structural recognition for floor plan interpretation. Int. J. Doc. Anal. Recogn. (IJDAR) **17**(3), 221–237 (2014)
8. de las Heras, L.-P., Terrades, O.R., Robles, S., Sánchez, G.: CVC-FP and SGT: a new database for structural floor plan analysis and its groundtruthing tool. Int. J. Doc. Anal. Recogn. (IJDAR) **18**(1), 15–30 (2015)
9. Gruber, T.R.: A translation approach to portable ontology specification. Knowl. Acquisition **5**, 199–220 (1993)
10. Harris, S., Seaborne, A.: SPARQL 1.1 Query Language (2013). http://www.w3.org/TR/sparql11-query/
11. Hitzler, P., Krötzsch, M., Parsia, B., Patel-Schneider, P.F., Rudolph, S.: OWL 2: Web Ontology Language (2012). http://www.w3.org/TR/owl2-primer
12. Horrocks, I., Patel-Schneider, P.F.., Boley, H., Tabet, S., Grosof, B., Dean, M.: SWRL: a semantic web rule language combining OWL and RuleML (2004). http://www.w3.org/Submission/SWRL
13. Kubias, A., Schenk, S., Staab, S., Pan, J.Z.: OWL SAIQL - an OWL DL query language for ontology extraction. In: Proceedings of the International Workshop on OWL: Experiences and Directions (2007)
14. Maillot, N.E., Thonnat, M.: Ontology based complex object recognition. Image Vis. Comput. **26**(1), 102–113 (2008)
15. Möller, M.: Fusion of spatial information models with formal ontologies in the medical domain, Ph.D. thesis, German Research Center for Artificial Intelligence (DFKI) (2011)
16. Nwogu, I., Zhou, Y., Brown, C.: An ontology for generating descriptions about natural outdoor scenes. In: IEEE International Conference on Computer Vision Workshops, pp. 656–663 (2011)
17. Pagels, M.: DAML - The DARPA Agent Markup Language (2006). www.daml.org

18. Piroi, F., Lupu, M., Hanbury, A., Sexton, A., Magdy, W., Filippov, I.: Clef-ip: retrieval experiments in the intellectual property domain. In: CLEF Evaluation Labs and Workshop (2012). No. Online Working Notes
19. Tongphu, S., Suntisrivaraporn, B., Uyyanonvara, B., Dailey, M.N.: Ontology-based object recognition of car sides. In: International Conference on Electrical Engineering/Electronics, Computer, Telecommunications and Information Technology, pp. 1–4 (2012)
20. Weber, M., Langenhan, C., Roth-Berghofer, T., Liwicki, M., Dengel, A., Petzold, F.: a.SCatch: semantic structure for architectural floor plan retrieval. In: Proceedings of the International Conference on Case-Based Reasoning, pp. 510–524 (2010)
21. Zhi, G.S., Lo, S.M., Fang, Z.: A graph-based algorithm for extracting units and loops from architectural floor plans for a building evacuation model. Comput. Aided Des. **35**(1), 1–14 (2003)

A System for Camera-Based Retrieval of Heterogeneous-Content Complex Linguistic Map

Bao Quoc Dang[1]([✉]), Phuong Le Viet[1], Muhammad Muzzamil Luqman[1], Mickael Coustaty[1], De Tran Cao[2], and Jean-Marc Ogier[1]

[1] L3i Laboratory, University of La Rochelle, La Rochelle, France
quoc_bao.dang@univ-lr.fr
[2] CICT, Can Tho University, Can Tho, Vietnam

Abstract. In this paper, we propose a camera-based document retrieval system using various local features as well as indexing methods. For feature extraction, we use well known features such as LLAH, SIFT, SURF and ORB that are invariant to image transformations and work well with images captured by cameras. In addition, we employ our new features, named as *Scale and Rotation Invariant Features (SRIF)*. SRIF is computed based on geometrical constraints between pairs of nearest points around a keypoint. Our systems are applied on dataset including 400 heterogeneous-content complex linguistic map images (huge size, 9800×11768 pixels resolution). The experimental results show that the system using SRIF is efficient in terms of retrieval time with 95.2% retrieval accuracy.

Keywords: Camera-based document image retrieval · Local features · Indexing

1 Introduction and Related Work

Recently, the search and the retrieval of document images has been used in a wide range of applications [1] such as: word searching [2], document similarity measurement [2], document image retrieval based on query by example (QBE), automatic document logo detection [3] and retrieving scanned documents in digital libraries [4] where each kind of data was used separately. This paper focus on heterogeneous-content complex linguistic map images retrieval. The maps contain both textual and graphical objects with complex layouts which poses difficulty in recognition, especially in camera-based applications.

Camera-based document image retrieval can be summarized as searching for the most relevant document images regarding the user's query that is captured by a digital camera [5–7]. This task creates challenging images for recognition, because captured images can be affected by uneven lighting, low resolution, motion blur and perspective distortion problems [8].

In last decade, several camera-based document image retrieval systems using local feature for real-time indexing and retrieval have been proposed. One of the

© Springer International Publishing AG 2017
B. Lamiroy and R. Dueire Lins (Eds.): GREC 2015, LNCS 9657, pp. 86–99, 2017.
DOI: 10.1007/978-3-319-52159-6_7

main advantages of local features is that they have been demonstrated to be distinctive, robust, and segmentation free [9,10].

It can be seen from the block diagram of an example system in Fig. 1 that there are two main phases for a camera-based document image retrieval system. These include the indexing phase and retrieval phase. Both of which share feature extraction step, which is comprised of keypoint detector and descriptor. For feature extraction and indexing phase, we usually have to choose suitable features and an indexing method to be used.

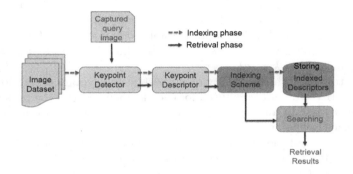

Fig. 1. Camera-based document image retrieval using local feature.

For local features, local keypoints are extracted in order to select parts of image that will be retained for the description part. These local points and regions are generally capable of reproducing similar levels of performances to human observers; in locating elementary features in a wide range of image types. Local keypoint detectors are used to detect interest regions that are invariant to a class of transformations (e.g. scaling, rotation and translation) so that for each detected region, which is usually represented as a keypoint, an invariant feature descriptor is built. Finally, these descriptors can be used as the basis to extract stable local image structures in a repeatable fashion and to encode them in a representation that is invariant to a range of image transformations, such as translation, rotation, scaling, and affine deformation [9,10].

Recently, Rusinol et al. [11] built a system for spotting graphical symbols in camera-acquired documents in real time. They used ORB (Oriented FAST and Rotated BRIEF) [12] to extract features vectors and FLANN frame work [13] for indexing the features vectors, as well as for retrieving and spotting query images. According to the authors, ORB features are fast and efficient for real-time application. In this system, the database stores important information which includes symbols and logos. In the retrieval phase, these objects are recognized and spotted in the captured query.

In camera-based textual document image retrieval, the method called Locally Likely Arrangement Hashing (LLAH) is known as an efficient method with regard to accuracy, time and scalability [14–17]. What is more important is that the authors proposed an efficient hashing technique, and LLAH has been shown superior to Geometric Hashing method concerning computational complexity [14,18].

LLAH feature extraction can be summarized as follows [19–21]. LLAH considers centroid of each word connected component as keypoints, which can be obtained even under perspective distortion, noise, and low resolution. A deep description on the method to obtain centroid of each word connected component can be found in [19]. From each keypoint P, the n nearest neighbor points around keypoint P are selected and organized clockwise. Then, all possible combination of m points among n are examined ($m < n$). From one arrangement combination of m points, the LLAH vector r is calculated based on a sequence of affine invariants calculated from all possible combinations of k points among m ($k = 3$ for similarity invariants, $k = 4$ for affine invariants and $k = 5$ for perspective invariants; $k < m$).

In order to reduce the sensibility of the system to keypoint extraction errors, multiple LLAH vectors are computed for each keypoint. As all the possible combinations of m points among n are examined, C_n^m LLAH vectors have to be built from each keypoint. As a consequence, the more LLAH vectors are built, the more processing time and memory consumption the system requires. Thus, n and m need to be suitably set depending on each system.

Aiming to deal with portions of document captured by camera, Takeda *et al.* [15] proposed an extension of the LLAH feature by adding some additional features which are based on the rank of k area ratios of the extracted word regions. In another work, they also proposed to improve the LLAH features by adding additional features based on rank of areas of words regions [17]. Similarly, Kise *et al.* [16] improved the LLAH feature by using the rank of k areas of letter regions and the query expansion method in order to cope with small document portions captured by camera-pen system [16].

Uchiyama *et al.* [22] proposed a camera-based system for map retrieval. They extracted intersection points from maps of Geographical Information Systems (GIS). Then, these intersection points are indexed and retrieved by applying LLAH.

Inspired by LLAH and the work from Su Yang [23], we have proposed a new feature called SRIF [24], which is computed based on geometrical constraints between pairs of nearest points around a keypoint. Moreover, our system works on small portions of documents. We validated it on a real-time document retrieval system with a textual document dataset. The work presented in [24] showed that SRIF outperformed LLAH from both the retrieval accuracy point of view and processing time point of view on textual document dataset.

In the current paper, we have taken our work on SRIF one step forward, and have performed new extensive experimentation to compare SRIF with the state-of-the-art feature descriptors including LLAH, SIFT, SURF and ORB. For achieving the latter, we have developed three new camera-based document retrieval systems based on SIFT, SURF and ORF features. Furthermore, we build a new dataset including 400 heterogeneous-content complex linguistic map images whose size are very large and have resolution of 9800×11768 pixels; for testing all methods. This new contribution enables us to better position our SRIF feature descriptor w.r.t. the state-of-the-art. We sincerely believe this work will be useful for the scientific community for choosing appropriate features for camera-based document image retrieval of various kinds of document images.

The rest of this paper is organized as follows. In Sect. 2, we present details about how SRIF works and also describe the camera-based systems using SIFT, SURF and ORB features. Section 3 presents the experimental results. Finally, the conclusion and future work are given in Sect. 4.

2   Camera-Based Document Image Retrieval System Using Local Features

In this section, we present details about camera-based document image retrieval system using SRIF, SIFT, SURF and ORB.

2.1   The System Using SRIF

The system using SRIF includes three main part: feature extraction, indexing phase and retrieval phase.

Feature extraction
Firstly, SRIF extracts centroids of word connected components as keypoints (as shown in Fig. 3). We can definitely employ centroids of letters as keypoints if needed. Then, SRIF feature vectors are extracted from each keypoint. It relies on the idea of using pairs of nearest constraint points around a keypoint (see Fig. 2). Let P be a keypoint, P_i and P_j two points coplanar with P. $|\overrightarrow{PP_i}|$ and $|\overrightarrow{PP_j}|$ denote the length of the two vectors $\overrightarrow{PP_i}$ and $\overrightarrow{PP_j}$, respectively, and θ_{ij} is the angle between these two vectors. It is obvious that the three values θ_{ij}, $L_{min_{ij}} = min(|\overrightarrow{PP_i}|/|\overrightarrow{PP_j}|, |\overrightarrow{PP_j}|/|\overrightarrow{PP_i}|)$ and $L_{max_{ij}} = max(|\overrightarrow{PP_i}|/|\overrightarrow{PP_j}|, |\overrightarrow{PP_j}|/|\overrightarrow{PP_i}|)$ are scale invariant and rotation invariant [23].

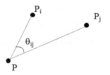

Fig. 2. Constraint between two point around one keypoint P.

Based on these scale and rotation invariant constraints between three points (as shown in Fig. 4), we propose two scale and rotation invariant ratios used for SRIF:

$$\theta_{ij}.L_{max_{ij}} \tag{1}$$

$$\theta_{ij}.L_{min_{ij}} \tag{2}$$

Image   Centroids of word CCs

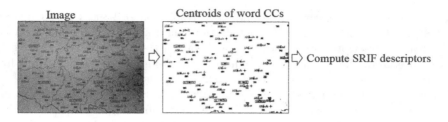

⇨ Compute SRIF descriptors

Fig. 3. Centroids of word connected components as keypoints

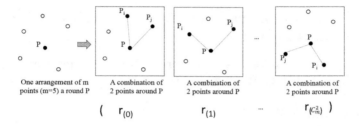

One arrangement of m   A combination of   A combination of   A combination of
points (m=5) a round P   2 points around P   2 points around P   2 points around P

$$(\quad r_{(0)} \qquad\qquad r_{(1)} \qquad \ldots \qquad r_{(C_m^2)} \quad)$$

Fig. 4. The arrangement of m points (m=5) and the sequence of new invariants (SRIF) calculated from all possible combinations of 2 points among m points.

From each keypoint P, n nearest neighbor points around P are selected and organized clockwise (e.g. $n = 6$). The nearest neighbor points are determined by using the Euclidean distance. After this, all possible combination of m points among n are examined with $m < n$ (e.g. $m = 5$ in Fig. 4). Then, from one arrangement combination of m points, the SRIF vector r is calculated based on a sequence of scale and rotation invariants calculated from all possible combinations of 2 points (constrained to P) among m points. Finally, each value of the SRIF vector, $r(i)$, is computed using invariant values: $\theta_{ij}.L_{max_{ij}}$ as presented in Eq. 1. As a result, the dimension of SRIF is C_m^2. To deal with keypoint extraction errors, C_n^m SRIF descriptors are computed for each keypoint similar to LLAH by using all possible combination of m points among n.

As SRIF feature vector is computed from m nearest neighbor points which are organized following a clockwise order. All points of m points are used as a starting point by examining all cyclic permutations of them in the retrieval phase to deal with rotation invariant. This is because SRIF feature vector of the retrieval algorithm does not match with SRIF feature vector in the storage algorithm due to rotations of camera-captured images. This takes more retrieval time because of the fact that the look-up in the hash table is done m times.

To overcome this problem, similar to the work from [19], we apply the method that could select the same starting points in both the storage and the retrieval processes. That is the point from which the maximum invariant is obtained by combining it with two clockwise succeeding points. In the case when there are two or more equivalent maximum values, succeeding clockwise invariant values of the starting point are used for comparison.

Indexing phase
Similar to LLAH, SRIF vectors (called r) can be indexed and retrieved very quickly using a hash table even if they are not stored in the hash table for checking distances of nearest neighbors [19]. Furthermore, this indexing scheme allows adding new documents into database without rebuilding all the database structure of indexes. Figure 5 presents the hashing strategy.

These performances rely on the use of integer feature vectors r, that are discretized and normalized as follows:

$$r(i) = trunc(r(i)) * 2 + round(r(i) - trunc(r(i))) \tag{3}$$

And the hash function is defined as follows [20]:

$$H_{index} = (\sum_{i=0}^{d-1} r_i q^i) \bmod H_{size} \tag{4}$$

where d is the number of dimensions of vector r, q is the level of quantization constant (e.g. $q = 17$), H_{size} is the size of hash table.

In order to add a new document into database, the system first extracts keypoints from centroids of word connected components. Then for each keypoint, all SRIF vectors are computed and indexed. As shown in Fig. 1, both indexing and retrieval share the feature extraction and use the same hash function (4).

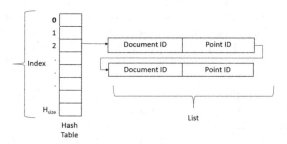

Fig. 5. The hash table structure.

Retrieval phase
Starting from a query image captured with a camera, keypoints are firstly extracted like in the indexing phase. Then for each keypoint, all SRIF vectors are computed and looked up in the indexing system, hash table (using hash function in 3) in order to get the list of document IDs related to each keypoint (Fig. 5). For each document in the retrieval result list, the number of votes for it in the voting table is incremented. After getting the voting result, the top-t documents with largest number of votes are selected as candidate results.

In order to check the correctly matched results in top-t returned documents. It must be ensured that whether or not there is a correct perspective transformation between query's keypoints and each document's keypoints. To validate this, RANSAC [25] is used. If no best transformation can be found, the number of votes is set to zero. Lastly, the document with majority of votes in top-t result documents is returned as the result. A correct retrieval result is validated if it has a correct document ID on one hand, and if it corresponds to the correct region of the document on the other hand.

2.2   The Systems Using SIFT, SURF and ORB

In this section, we describe the camera-based document image retrieval systems using one of three kinds of feature that involve SIFT [26], SURF [27] and ORB [12].

Feature extraction
The SIFT descriptor [26] is widely used for describing interest keypoints, because it is invariant to scaling, rotation and partially invariant to affine transform. First, the interest keypoints are detected by using the *D*ifference of Gaussians filter at different scales, then they are described based on the gradient orientations in sixteen 4×4 windows around the considered keypoint. Therefore, each SIFT feature vector is characterized by a 4×4 matrix of orientations of the intensity gradient. The orientation being quantized over eight values, the resulting SIFT feature vector is 128-dimensional, $S_i = (s_i^1, .., s_i^{128})$.

The second robust local detector and descriptor which we use in this work is the SURF [27]. SURF is developed to improve the runtime compared to SIFT, while it still obtains the good results. In SURF, the Hessian matrix and second order Gaussian derivative approximations are used to detect the interest points. Different from SIFT which uses the gradient, SURF uses the first order Haar wavelet responses in the two directions x and y. The typical SURF descriptor provide a vector of 64 dimensions.

The third local features that we use in this work is ORB. Different from SIFT and SURF, being a blob detector, ORB [12] is a corner detector and a binary descriptor. ORB computes corners by applying the modified version of FAST method [28] over a scale pyramid of the image. ORB also uses the modified version of BRIEF descriptor [29] with the oriented and scaled information of the keypoint. Therefore, it provides a binary descriptor with rotation and scale invariance. The binary descriptor of ORB describes the difference of intensities between pairs of pixels around the keypoint following a pair sampled on a smoothed patch. According to [29], in our experiments we chose the 256-dimensional bit-string, the patch size 31×31 and the smoothing kernel size 9×9.

Indexing phase
To able to work in the real-time with camera-based acquisition in our context, the computation time is an important concern. One of the solutions is reducing the high dimensionality of the feature descriptors.

For SIFT and SURF descriptors which are quite high dimensional descriptors, we apply Principal Components Analysis (PCA) to reduce the number of dimensions to 32-dimension vectors. As these features vectors are composed of a very large number of values, processing them means use of a lot of memory space and computation time. Valenzuela *et al.* [30] introduced a method using PCA to reduce the number of dimensions of SIFT and SURF vectors. PCA is used in the case that there is a large amount of numeric variables (observed variables) and it is desired to find a lower number of principal components, that will be responsible for higher variance in the observed variables. These principal components can be used as predictor variables in subsequent analysis. Valenzuela's experiments show that it is feasible to have an accurate low-dimensional feature vector after applying PCA.

Because the hashing framework, which is employed for SRIF and LLAH, is an exactly matching system. It can not be applied for indexing SIFT, SURF and ORB that need an approximate nearest neighbors matching systems. We decide to use FLANN [13] for SIFT and SURF features; LSH [31] for ORB features.

For the systems using SIFT and SURF, reduced dimension by applying PCA, they are indexed using FLANN frame work as described in [13]. The index constructed consist of a set of randomized kd-trees that are built by partitioning database descriptors. These kd-trees are searched in parallel in order to find nearest neighbor matching in high-dimensional spaces of query descriptors.

For the system using ORB, the binary feature vectors are indexed by LSH, whose index uses multi-probe LSH method from [31]. This indexing method is built on the well-known LSH technique and intelligently probes multiple buckets which are likely to contain query results in a hash table. It is more time and space efficient than ordinary LSH methods.

Retrieval phase
From a query image, feature vectors are extracted using SIFT, SURF or ORB. SIFT and SURF feature vectors are projected into PCA space before searching for their nearest neighbors stored in the indexing system (FLANN, LSH). After finding matched pairs of descriptors, each feature vector is matched with its nearest neighbor in database. Then, we filter the bad matching pairs by discarding those where the distance between two descriptors is less than a threshold Δ. Finally, the voting and validating phase are done similar to previous system by using RANSAC.

3   Experimentation

In this section we present dataset and the ground truth we built and we present the method used to evaluate the systems presented in this paper.

3.1   Dataset and the Ground Truth Generation

To evaluate the performance of all systems, we built a public dataset chosen from the CartoDialect French linguistic maps project, which is composed of 400 images

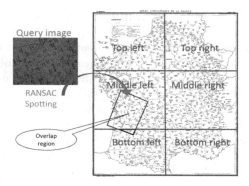

Fig. 6. Captured video from a map at six regions (red lines), the overlap (blue rectangle) between spotting region results and captured region from a query image. (Color figure online)

with a resolution of 9800×11768 pixels. Each map contains the phonetic symbols which describe the pronunciation of a word in different regions of France. All maps contain the same graphical elements which are region borders. Moreover, text density in each map is very sparse.

Each printed map was divided into 6 regions which are top left, top right, middle left, middle right, bottom left and bottom right (see Fig. 6 for details). The information of region is also used for validating the correct spotting in retrieval phase by dividing the database images into 6 regions with the same way. One video was recorded at each region. Documents were captured without rotations. The IPEVO VZ-1 HD document camera was used for recording the videos. It was fixed at 15 cm above surface of the captured document. The resolution of the frames of the captured video was 1024×768. This dataset is made publicly available for academic research purposes[1].

For each video, we selected the first 15 frames. To validate the rotation invariance, we also rotated each frame by an angle of 0, 90, and 180°. We choose two specific angle because it does not affect too much the keypoints which were extracted by a connected component (CC) extraction algorithm. There were 2400 captured videos, and the total number of queries in the ground truth is 36000.

3.2   Experimental Protocol and the Evaluation Measure

In order to evaluate all methods we measured the retrieval accuracy and the average retrieval time. For each video, we evaluated the retrieval accuracy called as the *video retrieval accuracy*. For this evaluation, 15 frames were extracted from each video, and each frame was rotated by an angle of 0, 90, or 180° before going to the retrieval phase. If number of correctly retrieved frames are greater than

---

[1] It can be downloaded from http://navidomass.univ-lr.fr/SRIFDataset/.

50% of total frames (15 frames) extracted from the video, video was considered as successful. Otherwise video was considered as failed. This threshold ensures that it is the majority returned result. Finally, videos retrieval accuracy is the ratio between the number of correct retrieval videos and the total of 2400 videos from the ground truth.

To validate the correct region, first RANSAC is applied so that we can obtain the spotting region of query image in the returned document through perspective transformation. Next, the overlap between the ground-truth region (where query image was captured) and the spotting region is calculated. The frame is considered as a correct retrieval result if the area of the overlap is more than 60% of the area of the spotting region otherwise it is considered as an incorrect result. An example of the overlap region validation is shown in Fig. 6.

LLAH and SRIF shared the same keypoint extraction approach which is based on the extraction of centroids of word connected components and share the indexing framework. We also used the method in [32] to discard the borders in the maps and to extract centroids of word CCs. Besides, small CCs which are noise were discarded. LLAH was tested with three invariants that are affine (LLAH-Affine), perspective (LLAH-Perspective) and similarity (LLAH-Similarity) invariant. For SRIF, LLAH-Affine, and LLAH-Similarity we set $n = 7$, $m = 6$ without adding additional features. For LLAH-Perspective n and m are set equaling to 8, 7 respectively. RIF was applied with invariant values: $\theta_{ij}.L_{max_{ij}}$ without adding additional features. $H_{size} = 10^{17}$, $t = 10$ for selecting top-t of best candidate retrieval results. To avoid collisions in the hash table wet set $q = 15$ for LLAH Affine and SRIF, $q = 3$ for LLAH Similarity, and $q = 2$ for LLAH-Perspective.

For SURF, SIFT and ORB extraction from the indexing phase, all maps are resized by a scale factor of 0.4 for reducing the resolution because of the large resolution of images. To filter the bad matching pairs the threshold Δ is set to 100, 0.1 and 45 for SIFT, SURF and ORB respectively. The indexing frame work (FLANN, LSH) for SIFT, SURF, ORB, we employ ones integrated with OpenCV library version 2.9. Our systems were implemented on a 64 GB RAM Linux machine running in C extended C++ environment with a single thread.

3.3 Experimental Results

The experimental results are shown in Table 1. It can be seen that the best performance method in terms of accuracy retrieval is SIFT-PCA-FLANN with 99.0%, and SRIF is the best in terms of retrieval time with 0.28 s/query. SRIF was the second highest in terms of accuracy retrieval with 95.2%. The third highest accuracy retrieval was LLAH-Similarity method with 94.5% and 0.38 s/query.

LLAH-Affine and LLAH-Perspective got the lowest accuracy retrieval. Accuracy retrieval of SURF-PCA-FLANN and ORB-LSH is approximately around 92%, but time retrieval of SURF-PCA-FLANN and ORB-LSH is quite slow (5.43 s/query and 11.37 s/query respectively).

With the same indexing frame work, but SURF-PCA-FLANN was slower than SIFT-PCA-FLANN in retrieval phase. This is because number of extracted

Table 1. The testing results

Method	Videos retrieval accuracy				Retrieval time			
	0°	90°	180°	Avg	0°	90°	180°	Avg
SRIF	95.7%	95.4%	94.6%	95.2%	0.28	0.28	0.29	**0.28**
LLAH-Similarity	95.0%	94.5%	93.9%	94.5%	0.38	0.37	0.39	0.38
LLAH-Affine	81.7%	80.8%	80.5%	81.0%	0.64	0.62	0.59	0.62
LLAH-Perspective	16.5%	15.7%	15.2%	15.8%	1.0	1.2	1.1	1.1
SIFT-PCA-FLANN	99.0%	99.1%	99.0%	**99.0%**	1.57	1.54	1.53	1.55
SURF-PCA-FLANN	92.6%	92.7%	91.9%	92.4%	5.61	5.41	5.27	5.43
ORB-LSH	92.7%	92.5%	92.4%	92.5%	11.50	11.20	11.40	11.37

Table 2. Total number of descritors indexed

Method	# of descriptors
LLAH	17,578,908
SRIF	17,578,908
SIFT-PCA-FLANN	16,558,819
SURF-PCA-FLANN	34,409,054
ORB-LSH	8,884,042

SURF descriptors are more than number of extracted SIFT descriptors, which is more than double (as shown in Table 2). It can be seen from the Table 2 that number of ORB descriptors is the smallest but ORB-LSH method got too low time retrieval (11.7 s/query) with LSH indexing frame work. Conversely, number of SRIF descriptors is largest but it was the fastest method that thanks to the efficient hashing index.

Both LLAH and SRIF use the same hashing method with the same number of descriptors. But retrieval time of SRIF is faster than LLAH. It proves that SRIF descriptors are more distinctive than LLAH descriptors, which can make collisions in the hash table reduce.

4   Conclusion

We have presented camera-based document image retrieval system using SRIF and LLAH with hashing index. In addition we have described the other systems using SIFT, SURF and ORB with FLANN and LSH indexing. The experimental results show that SRIF can correctly deal with the context of heterogeneous-content in document images. Furthermore SRIF with hashing index is promising from the retrieval accuracy point of view with retrieval accuracy 95.2%.

In the future, we are going to evaluate our systems on other datasets. We will also improve our new features (SRIF) in order to investigate into "generic descriptors" for information spotting in huge repositories of scanned document images.

We working on building a camare-based system for phonetic-symbol spotting on the complex liguistic maps dataset.

Acknowledgment. This work has been partially supported by the LabEx PERSY-VAL Lab (ANR-11-LABX-0025), by the CNRS PEPS Project CartoDialect, by the Program 165 of Vietnamese government by the ECLATS project funded by the French National Research Agency (ANR) under the grant ANR-15-CE-380002. The authors would like to thank Ms. MARWA MANSRI and Ms. TRAN HUYNH LE who helped us to construct the dataset and ground truth.

References

1. Kokare, M.B., Shirdhonkar, M.: Document image retrieval: an overview. Int. J. Comput. Appl. **1**, 114–119 (2010)
2. Niyogi, D., Srihari, S.N.: Use of document structure analysis to retrieve information from documents in digital libraries. In: Electronic Imaging 1997. International Society for Optics and Photonics, pp. 207–218 (1997)
3. Zhu, G., Doermann, D.: Automatic document logo detection. In: Ninth International Conference on Document Analysis and Recognition, ICDAR 2007, vol. 2, pp. 864–868. IEEE (2007)
4. Srihari, S.N., Shetty, S., Chen, S., Srinivasan, H., Huang, C., Agam, G., Frieder, O.: Document image retrieval using signatures as queries. In: Second International Conference on Document Image Analysis for Libraries, DIAL 2006, 6-pp. IEEE (2006)
5. Liu, Q., Liao, C.: PaperUI. In: Iwamura, M., Shafait, F. (eds.) CBDAR 2011. LNCS, vol. 7139, pp. 83–100. Springer, Heidelberg (2012). doi:10.1007/978-3-642-29364-1_7
6. Takeda, K., Kise, K., Iwamura, M.: Real-time document image retrieval on a smartphone. In: 2012 10th IAPR International Workshop on Document Analysis Systems (DAS), pp. 225–229. IEEE (2012)
7. Hull, J.J., Erol, B., Graham, J., Ke, Q., Kishi, H., Moraleda, J., Van Olst, D.G.: Paper-based augmented reality. In: 17th International Conference on Artificial Reality and Telexistence, pp. 205–209. IEEE (2007)
8. Liang, J., Doermann, D., Li, H.: Camera-based analysis of text and documents: a survey. IJDAR **7**, 84–104 (2005)
9. Tuytelaars, T., Mikolajczyk, K.: Local invariant feature detectors: a survey. Found. Trends Comput. Graph. Vis. **3**, 177–280 (2008)
10. Li, J., Allinson, N.M.: A comprehensive review of current local features for computer vision. Neurocomputing **71**, 1771–1787 (2008)
11. Rusiñol, M., Karatzas, D., Lladós, J.: Spotting graphical symbols in camera-acquired documents in real time. In: Lamiroy, B., Ogier, J.-M. (eds.) GREC 2013. LNCS, vol. 8746, pp. 3–10. Springer, Heidelberg (2014). doi:10.1007/978-3-662-44854-0_1
12. Rublee, E., Rabaud, V., Konolige, K., Bradski, G.: Orb: an efficient alternative to sift or surf. In: 2011 IEEE International Conference on Computer Vision (ICCV), pp. 2564–2571. IEEE (2011)
13. Muja, M., Lowe, D.G.: Fast approximate nearest neighbors with automatic algorithm configuration. VISAPP **2**, 331–340 (2009)

14. Nakai, T., Kise, K., Iwamura, M.: Use of affine invariants in locally likely arrangement hashing for camera-based document image retrieval. In: Bunke, H., Spitz, A.L. (eds.) DAS 2006. LNCS, vol. 3872, pp. 541–552. Springer, Heidelberg (2006). doi:10.1007/11669487_48

15. Takeda, K., Kise, K., Iwamura, M.: Real-time document image retrieval for a 10 million pages database with a memory efficient and stability improved LLAH. In: 2011 International Conference on Document Analysis and Recognition, pp. 1054–1058 (2011)

16. Kise, K., Chikano, M., Iwata, K., Iwamura, M., Uchida, S., Omachi, S.: Expansion of queries and databases for improving the retrieval accuracy of document portions: an application to a camera-pen system. In: Proceedings of the 9th IAPR International Workshop on Document Analysis Systems, pp. 309–316. ACM (2010)

17. Nakai, T., Kise, K., Iwamura, M.: Real-time retrieval for images of documents in various languages using a web camera. In: 10th International Conference on Document Analysis and Recognition, ICDAR 2009, pp. 146–150. IEEE (2009)

18. Wolfson, H.J., Rigoutsos, I.: Geometric hashing: an overview. Comput. Sci. Eng. **4**, 10–21 (1997)

19. Nakai, T., Kise, K., Iwamura, M.: Camera based document image retrieval with more time and memory efficient LLAH. In: Proceedings of the CBDAR, pp. 21–28 (2007)

20. Nakai, T., Kise, K., Iwamura, M.: Hashing with local combinations of feature points and its application to camera-based document image retrieval. In: Proceedings of the CBDAR 2005, pp. 87–94 (2005)

21. Iwamura, M., Nakai, T., Kise, K.: Improvement of retrieval speed and required amount of memory for geometric hashing by combining local invariants. In: Proceedings of the 18th British Machine Vision Conference (BMVC 2007), vol. 2, pp. 1010–1019 (2007)

22. Uchiyama, H., Saito, H., Servieres, M., Moreau, G.: AR GIS on a physical map based on map image retrieval using LLAH tracking. In: MVA, pp. 382–385 (2009)

23. Yang, S.: Symbol recognition via statistical integration of pixel-level constraint histograms: a new descriptor. IEEE Trans. Pattern Anal. Mach. Intell. **27**, 278–281 (2005)

24. Dang, Q., Luqman, M., Coustaty, M., N., Tran, C., Ogier, J.: Srif: scale and rotation invariant features for camera-based document image retrieval. In: 13th International Conference on Document Analysis and Recognition, ICDAR 2015, pp. 601–605. IEEE (2015)

25. Fischler, M.A., Bolles, R.C.: Random sample consensus: a paradigm for model fitting with applications to image analysis and automated cartography. Commun. ACM **24**, 381–395 (1981)

26. Lowe, D.G.: Distinctive image features from scale-invariant keypoints. Int. J. Comput. Vis. **60**, 91–110 (2004)

27. Bay, H., Tuytelaars, T., Gool, L.: SURF: speeded up robust features. In: Leonardis, A., Bischof, H., Pinz, A. (eds.) ECCV 2006. LNCS, vol. 3951, pp. 404–417. Springer, Heidelberg (2006). doi:10.1007/11744023_32

28. Rosten, E., Drummond, T.: Machine learning for high-speed corner detection. In: Leonardis, A., Bischof, H., Pinz, A. (eds.) ECCV 2006. LNCS, vol. 3951, pp. 430–443. Springer, Heidelberg (2006). doi:10.1007/11744023_34

29. Calonder, M., Lepetit, V., Strecha, C., Fua, P.: BRIEF: binary robust independent elementary features. In: Daniilidis, K., Maragos, P., Paragios, N. (eds.) ECCV 2010. LNCS, vol. 6314, pp. 778–792. Springer, Heidelberg (2010). doi:10.1007/978-3-642-15561-1_56

30. Valenzuela, R.E.G., Schwartz, W.R., Pedrini, H.: Dimensionality reduction through PCA over sift and surf descriptors. In: 11th IEEE Conference on Cybernetic Intelligent Systems, vol. 1, pp. 58–63 (2012)
31. Lv, Q., Josephson, W., Wang, Z., Charikar, M., Li, K.: Multi-probe LSH: efficient indexing for high-dimensional similarity search. In: Proceedings of the 33rd International Conference on Very large Data Bases, pp. 950–961. VLDB Endowment (2007)
32. Dang, Q., Luqman, M., Coustaty, M., Nayef, N., Tran, C., Ogier, J.: A multi-layer approach for camera-based complex map image retrieval and spotting system. In: 2014 4th International Conference on Image Processing Theory, Tools and Applications (IPTA), pp. 1–6. IEEE (2014)

Low Level, Segmentation and Structured Data

Towards the Alignment of Handwritten Music Scores

Pau Riba, Alicia Fornés$^{(\boxtimes)}$, and Josep Lladós

Computer Vision Center - Computer Science Department,
Universitat Autònoma de Barcelona, Bellaterra, Catalonia, Spain
{priba,afornes,josep}@cvc.uab.es

Abstract. It is very common to find different versions of the same music work in archives of Opera Theaters. These differences correspond to modifications and annotations from the musicians. From the musicologist point of view, these variations are very interesting and deserve study. This paper explores the alignment of music scores as a tool for automatically detecting the passages that contain such differences. Given the difficulties in the recognition of handwritten music scores, our goal is to align the music scores and at the same time, avoid the recognition of music elements as much as possible. After removing the staff lines, braces and ties, the bar lines are detected. Then, the bar units are described as a whole using the Blurred Shape Model. The bar units alignment is performed by using Dynamic Time Warping. The analysis of the alignment path is used to detect the variations in the music scores. The method has been evaluated on a subset of the CVC-MUSCIMA dataset, showing encouraging results.

Keywords: Optical music recognition · Handwritten music scores · Dynamic time warping alignment

1 Introduction

There are many Opera Theaters worldwide with a huge amount of handwritten music scores. Their archives contain the music scores of the different representations of Operas, Concerts and Ballets. For each one of these representations, many musicians (especially composers and conductors from the 18th–19th centuries) used to slightly modify the original music score with the aim of beautifying, easing the technical difficulties of some parts, etc. As a result, a particular music work could have many different versions due to the differences in the music notes, dynamics, tempo annotations, etc.

Indeed, many scholars focus their research on the analysis of these variations from the musicological point of view. For this purpose, they have to visually compare the different versions of the music composition, which is a time consuming task. Thus, a method that automatically detects the passages that contain variations could undoubtedly reduce their effort.

© Springer International Publishing AG 2017
B. Lamiroy and R. Dueire Lins (Eds.): GREC 2015, LNCS 9657, pp. 103–116, 2017.
DOI: 10.1007/978-3-319-52159-6_8

One solution could be to automatically recognize the handwritten music scores and then compare the resulting MIDI files. Although there are commercial products for Optical Music Recognition (OMR) of printed scores [1,2], the state of the art in handwritten music recognition [3,4] is still not mature enough. Nevertheless, there has been a huge advance in the recognition of isolated handwritten music symbols [5,6] as well as in on-line music recognition [7,8]. In the case of online OMR, the temporal information can effectively help in the recognition, and even some commercial products exist [9,10].

However, old handwritten music scores contain degradations, non-standard notation, and huge differences in the musicians' handwriting style. Thus, recognizing the music scores and comparing the MIDI files can not be taken into consideration yet. For this reason, we propose the alignment of music scores as an alternative. The main idea is to compare the two music scores from the visual appearance point of view, avoiding as much as possible its recognition.

In this paper we explore the use of a classical alignment technique for handwritten text and discuss the main difficulties and adaptations that should be taken into account when aligning music scores. The overview of the method is the following. First, braces and ties are removed. Then, music clefs and bar lines are detected. Afterwards, the Dynamic Time Warping (DTW) is used to align the bar units of the two music scores. Finally, the alignment path is analized for two reasons: first to detect the bar units that have been merged, and second, to detect the bar units that have been aligned with a high matching cost. Figure 1 shows the pipeline of the proposed approach.

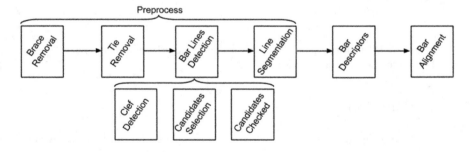

Fig. 1. Overview of the alignment process.

The rest of the paper is organized as follows. Section 2 describes the relevant music elements that have to be detected in the score. Section 3 describes the alignment of the bar units. Section 4 discusses the experimental results. Finally, conclusions and future work are drawn in Sect. 5.

2   Detection of Specific Music Elements

We assume that the input of our method is a binary image without staff lines. Concerning the staff lines removal, there are many methods in the literature devoted to this task, such as [11,12]. Indeed, according to the staff removal competitions held at ICDAR [13] and GREC [14], the performance of the current methods is extremely good.

So, the image without staff lines is cleaned by removing small blobs. The next step consists in detecting and removing certain elements that can generate confusion in the segmentation and alignment steps, such as the braces at the beginning of the document and the biggest ties. Then, the bar lines are detected and the different staffs are segmented.

2.1 Brace Removal

Braces appear at the beginning of the document and cover several staffs. They indicate that the music is polyphonic, composed of several staffs that are played in parallel, such as the music scores for piano, quartet, orchestra, choir, etc. (Fig. 2).

Given that braces can be easily misclassified as bar lines and increase the difficulties in staff segmentation, we propose to detect and delete the braces before the alignment. Thus, the brace detector analyzes the beginning of the staffs and, for each long (height) connected component, it applies a median filter with a vertical structuring element to detect a vertical long line. If the vertical cover several staffs, then it is considered a brace and removed from the image. Note that different music elements may belong to the same connected component. For example, in Fig. 9 several music clefs overlap the braces.

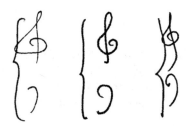

Fig. 2. Braces from different writers. Notice that some treble clefs overlap the braces.

The detailed steps are the following. First, we detect the beginning of the score, crop this region and compute the connected components. For each one of these elements, we must decide whether it is a brace or not. Following the musical notation theory, a brace must cross consecutive staffs. If there are elements satisfying these requirements, they are considered brace candidates. For these candidates, we apply a median filter with a thin vertical window to keep the almost vertical lines. However, braces might not be completely vertical and the lines that we get from the median filter will be split in to shorter lines. In order to join these lines, a dilatation with a vertical structural element is applied to the median filtered image. That dilation will join the different parts that can belong to the same brace. Finally, the skeleton is computed and each connected component is studied. For each one of these components, they are approximated as a straight line. If the line is long enough then it is considered a brace. Figure 3 shows the detection process of a Brace. The treble clef in this image is not fully connected and only the bottom part is shown.

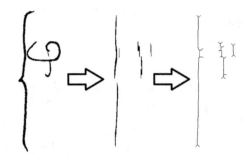

Fig. 3. From left to right: Original connected component, Median filtered image and final skeleton

Once all braces have been detected, they are deleted performing dilatations to the already approximated straight lines. This method is used instead of erasing the whole connected component because we should avoid deleting the clefs that can be next to the brace.

2.2   Tie Removal

Long ties are also common elements. These ties usually cross several bars, increasing the difficulties in line segmentation and bar unit detection (see Fig. 4). Also, misclassifying a tie may lead to incorrect music alignments, specially for the largest ones that will propagate these errors to several bar units.

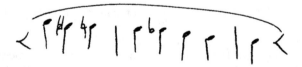

Fig. 4. Tie crossing 3 bars.

For this reason, we detect and remove these long ties by analyzing the aspect ratio of the long (width) connected components. Deleting smaller ones can erase parts of the symbols that are important for the alignment. Figure 5 shows an example where the beam is disconnected from the stems. These cases are easily confused with ties.

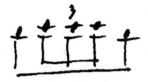

Fig. 5. Beam that can be confused with a tie.

The detection step is focused on connected components. We state that a component is a tie only if the aspect ratio and the width are bigger than a predefined threshold. This threshold prevents the algorithm to confuse cases like the ones in the Fig. 5 by asking the ties to be long enough.

2.3 Clef Detection

The detection of clefs at the beginning of each staff can be used to determine when a bar unit starts. When comparing music scores from different writers, it is common to find that a writer compresses the bar units more than others. As a result, the amount of bar units per line is different. In music notation, at the beginning of each staff, the clef and accidentals have to be written again. For this reason, these elements should not be taken into account when comparing the bar units from different writers.

To detect and recognize the clefs, the beginning of each staff is described using the Blurred Shape Model (BSM) [15], which can be considered as a weighed zoning descriptor. The BSM encodes the probability of pixel densities of image regions. The image is divided in a grid of n x m equal-sized subregions. Each bin receives votes from the foreground pixels in the image region, and also from the neighboring bins. In other words, each foreground pixel contributes to the density measure of its bin and its neighboring ones. This contribution is weighted according to the distance to the center of each bin.

For clef detection we follow the same procedure as for brace detection. First, an image region is cropped at the beginning of the staff. Afterwards, a morphological closing is performed to join small elements in the same connected component. If these components are big enough then they are considered a clef candidate. Then the BSM descriptor is computed and compared to a dataset of music clefs from different authors, which is described in [15]. Figure 6 shows some examples of this dataset.

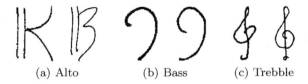

(a) Alto   (b) Bass   (c) Trebble

Fig. 6. Examples of clefs.

2.4 Bar Line Extraction

The bar lines are detected with two objectives. On the one hand, they are used to separate the bar units; on the other hand, they can be used to determine the number of voices in the musical score. Moreover, since the alignment is based on comparing the bar units of the music scores, the detection of bar lines is the most important step. A bad detection will lead to serious mistakes in the alignment. For example, Fig. 7 shows the problems that can come from the writing style of the author. In that image, it is easy to misclassify the stem of the note with a bar line.

Our bar detection consists in the following steps: bar line candidates and candidates test. These steps are described next.

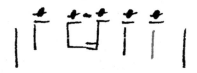

Fig. 7. The last stem (in red) can be confused as a bar line. (Color figure online)

Bar Line Candidates. First, a median filter is applied to detect the lines. Note that a bar line can overlap other elements. Every detected vertical line is marked as a candidate if it (almost) crosses all the staff and does not contain blobs at its extrema points (otherwise it is a note stem). Figure 8 shows the three steps: first the image, secondly the median filter and finally the chosen candidates.

Candidates Test. We check the consistency of the bar line candidates within their context. For example, we discard a bar line that is much shorter than the others, as well as a bar line that crosses only one staff in a two-voice music score.

For this purpose, we compute the length of all the detected bar lines and discard the outliers. First, we sort the candidates vertically in order to find the different lines of the document. These sorting can be done using the candidates centroid. When the lines have been detected, a set of outliers is computed.

Fig. 8. Bar lines detection pipeline.

Fig. 9. Detection of braces (in yellow), music clefs (in green) and bar lines (in red). The bar lines in blue color correspond to the virtual bar lines at the beginning or ending of each staff system. (Color figure online)

We consider that one candidate is an outlier if its length is very different from the candidates in the same line. We check whether some short lines could be vertically joined. Otherwise, they are finally rejected. Afterwards, the lines are checked to be truly separated. If a whole line is completely inside another, it is considered as an error, and all their candidates are deleted. Finally every bar is checked to be wide enough.

We would like to remark that virtual bar lines are added at the beginning and ending of each staff, just in case the musician forgot to draw them.

2.5 Staff Segmentation

The next step consists in segmenting the staffs. This is a critical step for elements that appear between the two staffs. For example, Fig. 10 shows some annotations and dynamics that can appear between two staffs. In such cases, the system has to decide which components belong to each staff.

Fig. 10. Line segmentation problems in red color. (Color figure online)

First the straight line that crosses through the middle point between staffs is computed. Afterwards, for every connected component that has been cut by that line is analysed. There are two possibilities:

- If the element crosses both staffs, then it is split in two. Thus, the component will be divided by the place of minimum width.
- Otherwise, the element will be assigned to the staff closer to the center of mass of the element.

3   Bar Alignment

The bar alignment can be divided in two stages: bar unit representation and bar alignment. These steps are described next.

3.1   Bar Unit Representation

For every bar unit, the vertical blank spaces are deleted because the space between notes can vary a lot between different authors. Next, the Blurred Shape Model descriptor is computed. The grid of the descriptor has been empirically set to 5 vertical and 50 horizontal divisions. These steps are shown in Fig. 11.

(a) Original   (b) No blank   (c) Descriptor

Fig. 11. Bar unit description.

3.2   Bar Unit Alignment

Once we have a descriptor for every bar unit, we can start aligning two music sheets, namely A and B. For this purpose, the Dynamic Time Warping (DTW) with Sakoe-Chiba band algorithm is used [16].

The DTW algorithm was originally proposed by Kruskal and Liberman for putting audio samples into correspondence. DTW is able to warp the time axis in order to optimize the best alignment between two signals. In addition, DTW can handle samples of different length avoiding resampling.

Let us define the DTW distance of two time series $C = x_1..x_M$ and $Q = y_1..y_N$ as $DTWCost(C, Q)$ (see Fig. 12(a)). For this purpose, a matrix

$D(i, j)$ (where $i = 1..M, j = 1..N$) of distances is computed using dynamic programming:

$$D(i, j) = min \left\{ \begin{array}{l} D(i, j-1) \\ D(i-1, j) \\ D(i-1, j-1) \end{array} \right\} + d2(x_i, y_j) \qquad (1)$$

$$d2(x_i, y_j) = x_i - y_j \qquad (2)$$

Performing backtracking along the minimum cost index pairs (i, j) starting from (M, N) yields the warping path (Fig. 12(b)). Finally, the matching cost is normalized by the length Z of this warping path:

$$DTWCost(C, Q) = D(M, N)/Z \qquad (3)$$

The creation of this path is the most important part of their comparison: it determines which points match (Fig. 12(c)) and are to be used to calculate the distance between the time series.

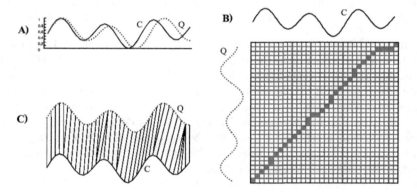

Fig. 12. An example of DTW alignment (extracted from [17]) (a) Samples C and Q. (b) The matrix D with the optimal warping path in grey color. (c) The resulting alignment.

In case of music alignment, each cell represents the matching cost of the bar units. Since we have a n-dimensional feature vector (in our case, n=5), the aligning cost stored in each cell of the matrix is computed using the square of the Euclidean distance of the BSM descriptors. Formally, if $f_k(a_i)$ corresponds to the k-th feature of the column i of the image A, and $f_k(b_j)$ corresponds to the k-th feature of the column j of the image B, the matching distance $DTWCost(A, B)$ is calculated using the same equations as in Kruskal's method, but instead of the Eq. 2, the computation of $d2$ will be the sum of the squares of the differences between individual features:

$$d2(x_i, y_j) = \sum_{k=1}^{5} (f_k(a_i) - f_k(b_j))^2 \tag{4}$$

Once the DTW alignment is applied, we focus on the backtracking path along the bars. These values indicate the aligning cost of each pair of bar units. We can consider the backtracking path as a first rough alignment. Then, every problematic alignment is studied. There are two different cases to consider:

- The backtracking path is following a diagonal movement although the matching cost is very high. This case means that the two bar units to be compared are very different (e.g. they contain different music notes). Then, the system marks these two bar units to be shown to the scholar.
- The paths are not following a diagonal movement (i.e. vertical or horizontal movement). It means that one bar unit in A is matching two or more bar units in B or vice-versa. This case can appear due to two reasons:
  - The musician (by mistake or deliberately) added or deleted a bar unit. The system marks these bar units.
  - The system could not detect a bar line (or the musician forgot to draw a bar line). This kind of mistakes have to be avoided as much as possible.

In order to decide whether two bar units should be joined, we compute the mean distance between the bar unit in A and the two bar units in B. Afterwards, we compute the same distance but joining both bar units (this means that we compute the joined BSM descriptor of the two bar units in B). If the second distance is smaller, then we consider that the bar units should be joined and we remove the bar line in the middle. Notice that this decision tends to delete a correct bar line in A whenever a bar line is not detected in B. Contrary, if this second distance is higher, then the algorithm considers that the musician added one extra bar unit and marks this difference.

In this way, every variation between the two music scores is marked and notified to the musicologist.

4   Results

For the experiments, we have selected a subset of the CVC-MUSCIMA dataset [18]. Concretely, we have selected 5 music works written by 8 different musicians (which means that we have 8 different versions). These music scores vary in length, number of voices, etc. For each one of these documents, we have created a ground-truth. Each bar line has an identifier number, corresponding to the order of appearance in the score (see the green numbers in Fig. 13).

These identifier numbers are consistent for the different versions. For example, in Fig. 14, a musician has merged several bar units (missing one bar line), so the ground-truth indicates this issue by using the correct identifier.

Fig. 13. Ground-truth example. (Color figure online)

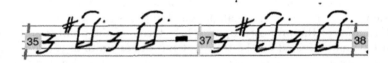

Fig. 14. Ground-truth correction. The musician forgot to write the bar line n.36.

4.1 Bar Lines Extraction Evaluation

The first experiment consists in evaluating the performance of the bar line extraction proposed in Sect. 2.4. It is important to validate it because the alignment highly depends on a correct bar line extraction.

Table 1 shows the performance of the proposed technique. Precision is the fraction of retrieved instances that are relevant and Recall is the fraction of relevant instances that are retrieved. From the results we can conclude that the bar detection is not perfect although accurate enough for the next stage. It is important to remark that the alignment is able to detect that two bar units should be joined.

Table 1. Bar lines detection

Metric	Result
Precision	89.383 %
Recall	95.327 %

Figure 15a shows an example of False Positive (FP) whereas Fig. 15b presents the opposite case, a False Negative (FN).

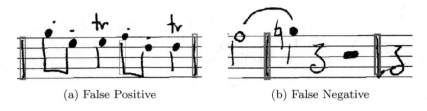

    (a) False Positive   (b) False Negative

Fig. 15. Bar descriptor

4.2 Alignment Evaluation

The next experiment evaluates the performance of the alignment approach. This evaluation has been done comparing the bar line identifiers of every pair of aligned music sheets with the ones in the ground-truth. Since there are 8 versions of 5 music works, we have run the alignment 140 times (5 * 28). Table 2 presents the performance of the proposed approach in terms of the number of corrected matched bar units divided by the total amount of bar units in the music score.

Figure 16 shows the same passage from two musicians. Notice that the second writer made a mistake in bar unit 36. In the image, the green numbers correspond to the identifier in the ground truth, whereas the red ones are the ones proposed by the alignment algorithm. Obviously, the bar unit number 37 is a combination of the 36 and 37 ones. The algorithm detects that there is indeed a variation, marking these bar units and notifying the scholar.

Table 2. Alignment results.

Metric	Result
Accuracy	88.743 %

Fig. 16. Detection of a variation between two musical scores. (Color figure online)

5   Conclusion and Future Work

In this paper, we have proposed a music score alignment method for detecting variations in music sheets. The method is based on the detection and alignment of bar units using the classical Dynamic Time Warping. We have analyzed the main difficulties and adaptations that must be performed.

The experimental results are encouraging. Thus, we could conclude that music alignment can be seen as a semi-blind tool from the optical music recognition point of view, but with the ability to detect variations between two music scores.

Future work will be focused on analyzing the performance of the bar unit detection. Moreover, we will focus on the detection of variations inside each bar unit. This detection will be done element by element such as notes or dynamics. For this purpose, we plan to use more powerful techniques such as graph-based techniques.

Acknowledgment. This work has been partially supported by the Spanish project TIN2015-70924-C2-2-R, the European project ERC-2010-AdG-20100407-269796 and the *Ramon y Cajal* Fellowship RYC-2014-16831.

References

1. Photoscore. http://www.neuratron.com/photoscore.htm
2. Sharpeye. http://www.visiv.co.uk/
3. Rebelo, A., Fujinaga, I., Paszkiewicz, F., Marcal, A., Guedes, C., Cardoso, J.: Optical music recognition: state-of-the-art and open issues. Int. J. Multimedia Inf. Retrieval **1**(3), 173–190 (2012)
4. Fornés, A., Sánchez, G.: Analysis and recognition of music scores. In: Doermann, D., Tombre, K. (eds.) Handbook of Document Image Processing and Recognition, pp. 749–774. Springer, London (2014)
5. Rebelo, A., Capela, G., Cardoso, J.S.: Optical recognition of music symbols: a comparative study. Int. J. Doc. Anal. Recogn. **13**(1), 19–31 (2010)
6. Fornés, A., Lladós, J., Sánchez, G., Karatzas, D.: Rotation invariant hand drawn symbol recognition based on a dynamic time warping model. Int. J. Doc. Anal. Recogn. **13**(3), 229–241 (2010)
7. Miyao, H., Maruyama, M.: An online handwritten music symbol recognition system. IJDAR **9**(1), 49–58 (2007)
8. Calvo-Zaragoza, J., Oncina, J.: Recognition of pen-based music notation with probabilistic machines. In: Proceedings of the 7th International Workshop on Machine Learning and Music, Barcelona, Spain (2014)
9. Myscript music. http://myscript.com/technology/music
10. Staffpad. http://www.staffpad.net/
11. Dalitz, C., Droettboom, M., Pranzas, B., Fujinaga, I.: A comparative study of staff removal algorithms. IEEE Trans. Pattern Anal. Mach. Intell. **30**(5), 753–766 (2008)
12. dos Santos Cardoso, J., Capela, A., Rebelo, A., Guedes, C., Pinto, K.: Staff detection with stable paths. IEEE Trans. Pattern Anal. Mach. Intell. **31**(6), 1134–1139 (2009)

13. Visani, M., Kieu, V.C., Fornés, A., Journet, N.: ICDAR 2013 music scores competition: staff removal. In: 2013 12th International Conference on Document Analysis and Recognition (ICDAR), pp. 1407–1411. IEEE (2013)
14. Fornés, A., Dutta, A., Gordo, A., Lladós, J.: The 2012 music scores competitions: staff removal and writer identification. In: Kwon, Y.-B., Ogier, J.-M. (eds.) GREC 2011. LNCS, vol. 7423, pp. 173–186. Springer, Heidelberg (2013). doi:10.1007/978-3-642-36824-0_17
15. Escalera, S., Fornés, A., Pujol, O., Radeva, P., Sánchez, G., Lladós, J.: Blurred Shape Model for binary and grey-level symbol recognition. Pattern Recogn. Lett. **30**(15), 1424–1433 (2009)
16. Sakoe, H., Chiba, S.: Dynamic programming algorithm optimization for spoken word recognition. IEEE Trans. Acoust. Speech Sig. Process. **26**(1), 43–49 (1978)
17. Keogh, E., Ratanamahatana, C.: Exact indexing of dynamic time warping. Knowl. Inf. Syst. **7**(3), 358–386 (2005)
18. Fornés, A., Dutta, A., Gordo, A., Lladós, J.: CVC-MUSCIMA: a ground truth of handwritten music score images for writer identification and staff removal. Int. J. Doc. Anal. Recogn. **15**(3), 243–251 (2012)

Improving Fuzzy Multilevel Graph Embedding Technique by Employing Topological Node Features: An Application to Graphics Recognition

Hana Jarraya[1]($\boxtimes$), Muhammad Muzzamil Luqman[2], and Jean-Yves Ramel[3]

[1] Computer Vision Center, Barcelona, Spain
hanajarraya@cvc.uab.es
[2] L3i Laboratory, University of La Rochelle, La Rochelle, France
muhammad_muzzamil.luqman@univ-lr.fr
[3] Laboratoire d'Informatique, Tours, France
jean-yves.ramel@univ-tours.fr

Abstract. The graphics recognition research community has been employing graphs, in one form or another, for at-least the last three decades. These data-structures have proven to be the most powerful representations for encoding the structural information of underlying data, for further processing. However, there is still a lack of tools and methods which could be employed to process these useful data-structures in an efficient manner. Graph embedding provides a solution for this problem. In this paper we present an improvement of the *Fuzzy Multilevel Graph Embedding (FMGE)* technique, by adding new topological node features, named *Morgan Index*. The experimental results on *GREC, Mutagenicity* and *Fingerprint* datasets from IAM graph database, illustrate improved results for the graph classification and graph clustering problems.

Keywords: Graphics recognition · Graph classification · Graph clustering · Explicit graph embedding · Topological node features · Morgan index

1 Introduction and Related Work

The Pattern Recognition (PR) in general and the Graphics RECognition (GREC) in particular, are generally approached by two big families of techniques: structural methods and statistical methods. The statistical methods generally extract information about the distribution of pixel intensities in underlaying images and represent it by numeric feature vectors. Where as the structural methods generally represent the images by a graph-based data structure and perform different operations directly on graphs such as graph matching and/or graph isomorphism [1].

Graphs are able to represent properties of graphics units in images and the relations between them at the same time. During the three last decades a

© Springer International Publishing AG 2017
B. Lamiroy and R. Dueire Lins (Eds.): GREC 2015, LNCS 9657, pp. 117–132, 2017.
DOI: 10.1007/978-3-319-52159-6_9

continuous interest in graph-based representations by the GREC community is observed [1–7, 18–20].

The high computational cost and the lack of mathematical tools defined in graph space are the limitations of graph-based methods. During the last 5 years Graph EMbedding (GEM) has emerged as a promising approach to address these limitations of graph-based methods. By encoding a graph into a numeric feature vector Graph EMbedding (GEM) permits the last works on the graph-based methods to employ the efficient computational tools of machine learning [1].

Recently many interesting works on Graph EMbedding (GEM) applied to Graphics Recognition (GREC) have been proposed. These works have been summarized and compared in [11]. [14] presents vector representations of graphs applied to recognition of symbols and letters. It presents an extension of the vector representation based on pattern frequency, which integrates labeling information. [15] presents a method that vectorizes a graphic symbol, encodes its topological and geometrical information by an attributed relational graph and computes a vectorial signature from this structural graph. It uses data adapted fuzzy intervals to address the noise sensitivity of graphs. Then it encodes the joint probability distribution of signatures by a Bayesian network, which serves as a mechanism for pruning irrelevant features and choosing a subset of interesting features from structural signatures of underlying symbol set. The Bayesian network is deployed in a supervised learning scenario for recognizing graphic symbols. [1] presents a Graph EMbedding (GEM) robust and error-tolerant method named as *Fuzzy Multilevel Graph Embedding (FMGE)*. It permits to embed attributed graphs with numeric as well as symbolic attributes on both nodes and edges, into numeric feature vectors by extracting graph level details, subgraph homogeneity details and elementary level details. The method has shown good results for many public graph datasets [1]. However, there is a lack of topological information in the feature vectors of FMGE. Since, the main advantage of graphs comes from the fact that it represents a lot of relational information of images by its topology, we propose to extend FMGE. In this paper we improve FMGE by extracting and encoding more information on the topology of the graphs. For the latter, we use the Morgan Index [22] based Topological Node Features (TNF) from [8].

The rest of this paper is organized as follows. In Sect. 2, we introduce the definitions and notations used in the paper. In Sect. 3, we present details on the proposed method of extension of FMGE by Topological Node Features (TNF). In Sect. 4, we present the details on the experimentation and a discussion on the obtained results. Section 5 presents the conclusion and future directions of work.

2   Definitions and Notations

This section introduces the definitions [1, 8] and notations, which we have used in the paper.

Attributed graph (AG): Let A_V and A_E denote the domains of possible values for attributed vertices and edges respectively. These domains are assumed to include a special value that represents a null value of a vertex or an edge. In this paper, the term attributed graph is used to refer to an undirected attributed graph, unless explicitly specified. An attributed graph AG over (A_V, A_E) is defined to be a four-tuple:

$$AG = (V, E, \mu^V, \mu^E)$$

where V is a set of vertices, $E \subseteq V \times V$ is a set of edges, $\mu^V : V \mapsto A_V^k$ V is function assigning k attributes to vertices and, $\mu^E : E \mapsto A_E^l$ E is a function assigning l attributes to edges.

Graph order: The order of a graph $AG = (V, E, \mu^V, \mu^E)$ is given by $|V|$ i.e. the number of vertices in AG. Let AG_1 and AG_2 be two attributed graphs, then:

$$AG_1 \text{ is smaller than } AG_2 \Leftrightarrow |V_1| < |V_2|$$
$$AG_1 \text{ and } AG_2 \text{ are equal ordered } \Leftrightarrow |V_1| = |V_1|$$
$$AG_1 \text{ is bigger than } AG_2 \Leftrightarrow |V_1| > |V_2|$$

Graph size: The size of a graph $AG = (V, E, \mu^V, \mu^E)$ is given by $|E|$ i.e. the number of edges in AG. Let AG_1 and AG_2 be two attributed graphs, then:

$$AG_1 \text{ is thinner than } AG_2 \Leftrightarrow |E_1| < |E_2|$$
$$AG_1 \text{ and } AG_2 \text{ are equal sized } \Leftrightarrow |E_1| = |E_2|$$
$$AG_1 \text{ is thicker than } AG_2 \Leftrightarrow |E_1| > |E_2|$$

Node degree: The degree of a vertex (or node) V_i in graph $AG = (V, E, \mu^V, \mu^E)$ refers to the number of edges connected to V_i. If AG is a directed graph then each of its nodes has an in-degree and an out-degree associated to it. The in-degree refers to the number of incoming edges and out-degree refers to the number of outgoing edges for a node. Generally, the terms densely connected graph and sparsely connected graph are used for abstractly categorizing a graph on the basis of its node degrees.

Explicit graph embedding: Explicit graph embedding maps a graph to a point in suitable vector space. It encodes the graphs by equal size vectors and produces one vector per graph. Mathematically, for a given graph $AG = (V, E, \mu^V, \mu^E)$ explicit graph embedding is a function ϕ, which maps graph AG from graph space G to a point $(f_1, f_2, \ldots, f_n)$ in n dimensional vector space R^n. It is given as

$$\phi : G \mapsto R^n$$

$$AG \mapsto \phi(AG) = (f_1, f_2, \ldots, f_n)$$

n-Neighborhood: Given a graph G with node v, a nNeighbourhood $nN(v, n)$ is a subgraph:

$$G' = (V', E')$$

where V' is the set of nodes in G that can be reached within n steps from v, and $E' = (V'xV') \cap E$ [8].

Morgan Index (MI): The Morgan Index is a powerful TNF which calculates a hash value from a graph's topology [22]. Originally used to characterize chemical structures, it has recently been effectively applied to graph isomorphism [21]. Given an attributed graph $AG = (V, E, \mu^V, \mu^E)$, a node $v \in AG$, [8] defines the Morgan Index of v as:

$$MI_i(v) = \begin{cases} feature(v) = node\_degree(v), & \text{if } i = 0 \\ \Sigma_u MI_{i-1}(u), & \text{otherwise} \end{cases}$$

where u is a node adjacent to v, the *feature* function is the *node degree*, i is the level of Morgan Index and $MI_{i-1}(u)$ is the summation of the adjacents nodes degree of v in previous iteration $i - 1$ of the propagation MI technique.

3   Proposed Method

Fuzzy Multilevel Graph Embedding (FMGE) is an unsupervised method for explicit embedding of directed and undirected attributed graphs with many numeric as well as symbolic attributes on both nodes and edges (which represent a very general super class of graphs), into feature vectors [1]. FMGE employs fuzzy logic for addressing the noise sensitivity of graph based representations whilst achieving a simple and straight forward embedding of topological, structural and attribute information of a graph into a low-dimensional numeric feature vector. FMGE embeds an attributed graph into a feature vector by extracting graph level details (graph order and graph size), sub-graph homogeneity details (node degree, node attributes resemblance for edges and edge attributes resemblance for nodes) and elementary level details (node attributes and edge attributes).

Based on the work presented in [8], Dahm et al. have shown the performance of a set of advanced topological node features calculated from n-neighborhood sub-graphs. One of these techniques that significantly improve the effectiveness of sub-graph isomorphism problems is the *Morgan Index (MI)*. This feature is defined as *topological node feature (TNF)* value assigned to a node which encodes information about the local graph topology into a simple value. So, the main idea of our proposed method in this paper is to include more information on the topology of graph by using the Morgan's Index as advanced node attribute.

In this rest of this section, we first briefly introduced the details of FMGE technique. Then we present details on the new Topological Node Features (TNF) and finally the extension of $FMGE$ by using the TNF.

3.1   Fuzzy Multilevel Graph Embedding FMGE

FMGE method accepts a list of m attributed graphs as input and encodes their topological, structural and attribute details into m equal size feature vectors [1]. The resulting feature vector is named as *Fuzzy Structural Multilevel Feature Vector (FSMFV)*.

As input, the *FMGE* has m attributed graphs $(AG_1, \ldots, AG_e, \ldots, AG_m)$, where the eth graph is denoted by $AG_e = (V, E, \mu^V, \mu^E)$.

As output, the features vectors denoted by $(FSMFV_1, \ldots, FSMFV_m)$. The eth input graph AG_e is embedded into feature vector $FSMFV_e$:

$$AG_e \mapsto \phi(AG_e) = FSMFV_e$$

where $FSMFV_e$ is a point in n dimensional vector space R_n: $FSMFV_e = (f_{e1}, f_{e2}, \ldots, f_{en})$.

The embedding process is performed out in two steps. The first step is learning the *Fuzzy Bins* for each attribute using the training dataset. This unsupervised learning phase learns a set of fuzzy intervals for features linked to distribution analysis of the input graphs i.e. features for node degree, numeric node and edge attributes and the corresponding resemblance attributes. It refers each of them as an attribute i.

The ressemblance attributes are supplementary information added to the graph. It describes the ressemblance among the relationships associated to a primitive component. The node ressemblance attributes for edge is a new edge attribute. It encodes structural information ressemblance between a couple of nodes linked by an edge. The edge ressemblance attributes for node is a new node attribute. Given a node in a graph, the resemblance for the edges connected to this node is computed as the mean of the resemblances between all the pair of edges connected to this node. The calculation of the ressemblance attributes depends on the kind of the corresponding attribute, numeric or symbolic.

For symbolic node and edge attributes and the corresponding resemblance attributes, the unsupervised learning phase employs the modalities taken by an attribute i to build its proper crisp intervals. From these initial set of crisp intervals, we arrange them to build the set of fuzzy overlapping trapezoidal intervals for an attribute i. These intervals are used later to obtain a histogram related to the attribute i.

The second step in FMGE is the creation of the histograms. This graph embedding phase employs the learned fuzzy overlapping trapezoidal intervals for constructing fuzzy histogram for an attribute i for input graph AG_e. Each attribute i of AG_e has its own histogram. To full the histogram, first we calculate the membership degree of every modality or instance of the attribute i based on the trapezoidal function. Then, we sum the memberships for each fuzzy interval. The fuzzy histogram gives the required embedding of attribute i for constructing feature vector for a graph AG_e. Figure 1 outlines this part of this feature vector FSMFV.

Histogram of node degree h^d	Histograms of node attributes ressemblance h_d^{nr} and $h_1^{nr}, h_2^{nr}, ..., h_k^{nr}$	Histograms of edge attributes ressemblance h_d^{er} and $h_1^{er}, h_2^{er}, ..., h_k^{er}$

Fig. 1. Embedding of structural level information

For the case of symbolic attribute, every symbolic attribute j on the nodes and edges of a graph is embedded by a crisp histogram of the modalities of the attribute j. This is achieved during graph embedding phase, during which the cardinality of each modality that can be taken by attribute j, is encoded by exactly one numeric feature in the feature vector for a graph AG.

We can find more details about $FMGE$ in [1].

3.2   Topological N-Neighbourhood Feature

A TNF is calculated from graph topology as viewed from a particular node [8]. An n-Neighberhood of a node v is an induced subgraph formed from all the nodes that can be reached within n steps from v, noted $nN(v, n)$ as shown in Fig. 2.

For each graph node v, a unique nN may be created for each value $n = 1, 2, \ldots,$ m, where $nN(v, m) = G$ (the entire graph can be reached in m steps).

In the case of directed graphs, each nN is replaced by a pair of nNs, one for each direction of edges leaving the center node. Here, to calculate the Morgan

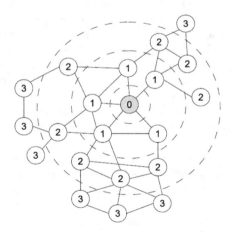

Fig. 2. Vizualisation of nN(v,n) at n = 0, 1, 2, 3 for the central (grey) node. The value of n at which each node is added to the nN, is displayed for all nodes. All nodes and edges within (but not crossing) the chosen dotted line make up an nN [8].

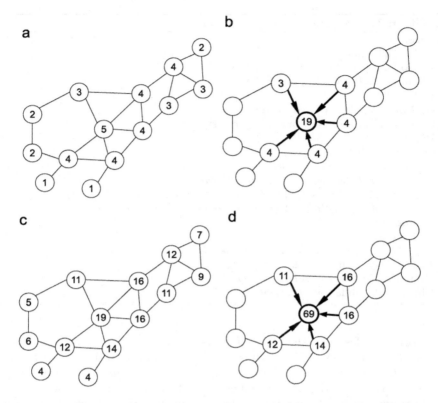

Fig. 3. The Summation Index propagation procedure to calculate the MI, shown for the degree TNF. (a) Node degrees, (b) propagating degrees, (c) SI=1 node degrees, (d) propagating SI=1 degrees [8].

Index, we present the propagation technique called the *Summation Index (SI)* as shown in Fig. 3, where the degree TNF is strengthened. Simply by taking the sum of the adjacent TNF values, each SI iteration encodes more distant topological information than the last. Given the initial node degrees in Fig. 3a, there are five unique TNF values. After only a single SI iteration, the number of unique TNF values has increased to 10. As the SI TNF values (one for each iteration) are numbers.

3.3 Extending FMGE with TNF

The Topological Node Features (TNF), once computed, are added to the nodes of the graph as a new attribute. By employing the $FMGE$ framework we propose to encode a graph into a feature vector.

Algorithm 1. Graph Embedding algorithm

Require:
1: Train, Valid and Test graphs datasets
2: list: MIL ={MorganIndexLevels}
3: list: $nbrCI$ ={nbrOfCrispIntervals}
Ensure:
4: list:$FSMFV\_list$ ={FSMFVectors}
5: list:$EvalResults\_list$=IncorrectClusterInstPercentage
6: **Begin:**
7: **for** $param_1$ in MIL **do**
8:     **for** $param_2$ in $nbrCI$ **do**
9:         $FuzzyInts$=LearningFuzzyInts($TrainDataSet$)
10:         $FSMFV\_list$=GraphEmbedding($FuzzyInts$, $ValidDataSet$)
11:         $EvalResults\_list$=Clustering&Validation ($ValidDataSet$)
12:     **end for**
13: **end for**
14: $BestParamComb$=ChooseBest($EvalResults\_list$)
15: $FuzzyInts$= LearningFuzzyInts ($TrainDataSet$)
16: GraphEmbedding($FuzzyInts$, $TestDataSet$)
17: Clustering&Validation ($TestDataSet$)

Algorithm 1 describes the different steps in detail. First we choose the parameters values: number of Fuzzy Bins and Morgan Index level. Then, we apply the $FMGE$ process on the valid graphs dataset with different parameters values. And, we do the clustering on the embedded features vectors. After, we evaluate the clustering and we choose the six first parameters that allows better result of clustering evaluation. We run the $FMGE$ technique with these six parameters on test graphs dataset. Then we apply clustering on the embedded vectors. Finally, while evaluation, we pick the $FMGE$ parameters that corresponds to the good evaluation clustering result.

The example shown in Fig. 4 descries the computation of the MI of level 2 of a center node colored in grey. Figure 4(a) represents a simple graph. Figure 4(b) calculates the node degree of all the nodes. Figure 4(c) illustrates the sub-graph $nN(v, 1)$ of the grey center node and calculates the MI of level 1. It's the sum of node degrees of its neighbors and the node degree of the grey node ($18 = 2 + 2 + 2 + 3 + 4 + 5$). Figure 4(d) illustrates the sub-graph $nN(v, 2)$ of the grey center node and calculates the MI of level 2. It's the sum of node degrees of the nodes 2 steps far from the grey node. These nodes belong to nN(v, 2) and the MI of level 1 of the grey node ($26 = 18 + 2 + 1 + 1 + 2 + 2$). As a result, we have the MI of the grey node is (18, 26).

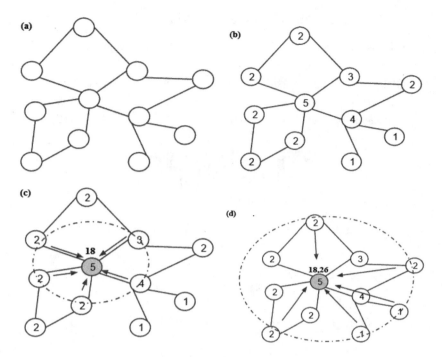

Fig. 4. Morgan Index computation. (a) simple graph (b) node degree graph (c) MI of level 1 related to the grey node calculated from nN(v, 1) sub-graph (d) MI of level 2 related to the grey node calculated from nN(v, 2) sub-graph

4   Experimentation

The experimentation was performed to evaluate the performance of the improved *FMGE* technique for the problems of graph classification and graph clustering, with an application to graphics recognition. We have employed standard public datasets [17] from the fields of graphic symbol recognition and object recognition. All experiments were run on a computer with an Intel core i5 Processor and 4 GB of RAM.

4.1   Graph Datasets

We will describe three *IAM* graph datasets, FingerPrint, GREC and Mutagenicity graphs. Table 1 presents more details about the graphs in these datasets.

Fingerprints are converted into graphs by filtering the images and extracting regions that are relevant (Fig. 5). In order to obtain graphs from fingerprint images, the relevant regions are binarized and a noise removal and thinning procedure is applied [17]. Ending and bifurcation points of the skeletonized regions

Table 1. IAM graph database

Dataset	Size			Classes	Sym:Num	Max	
	Train	Valid	Test			$\|V\|$	$\|E\|$
GREC	286	286	528	22	2 : 4	25	30
FingerPrint	500	300	2000	11	0 : 4	26	25
Mutagenicity	1500	500	2337	2	1 : 1	417	112

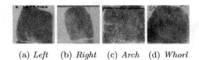

(a) *Left*   (b) *Right*   (c) *Arch*   (d) *Whorl*

Fig. 5. Fingerprint examples from the four classes.

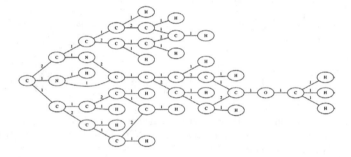

Fig. 6. Graph of the $C_{22}H_{18}N_2O_1$ molecule. The nodes are labeled correspondingly to chemical elements (C, H, N or O). The edges model the covalent links; their labels are equal to their numbers (Mutegenicity).

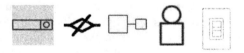

Fig. 7. A sample image of each distortion level (GREC).

are represented by nodes. Undirected edges are inserted to link nodes that are directly connected. Each node is labeled with a two-dimensional attribute giving its position. The edges are attributed with an angle denoting the orientation of the edge with respect to the horizontal direction.

Symbol images occur at five different distortion levels [17] to construct **GREC graphs**. For each distortion level one example of a drawing is given (Fig. 7). The result is thinned to obtain lines of one pixel width. Finally, graphs are extracted from images by tracing the lines from end to end and detecting intersections as well as corners. Ending points, corners, intersections and circles are represented by nodes and labeled with a two-dimensional attribute giving their position. The nodes are connected by undirected edges which are labeled as line or arc. An additional attribute specifies the angle with respect to the horizontal direction or the diameter in case of arcs.

Mutagenicity molecules are converted into graphs in a straightforward manner by representing atoms as nodes and the covalent bonds as edges as shown in Fig. 6. Nodes are labeled with the number of the corresponding chemical symbol and edges by the valence of the linkage [17].

4.2 Experimental Sets up and Results

Experimentation has been carried out on FingerPrint, GREC, Mutagenicity graphs. Clustering is generally performed in an unsupervised manner and normally for clustering tasks no separate learning set is available. The experimentation is simulated as the following steps: During a first pass on the graph data set, $FMGE$ learned fuzzy intervals for various numeric attributes in graphs and then during second pass on the same graph dataset it employed these fuzzy intervals for graph embedding.

A more sophisticated and advanced discretization technique has been employed for obtaining the initial set of crisp intervals for graph clustering and classification experimentations. This technique is based on the use of discretization technique proposed in the Weka library [24]. It gives a set of crisp intervals for underlying data which could be safely termed as equal frequency intervals. The resulting fuzzy intervals, which are calculated from the spread of the respective attribute's values, are true representative of the shape of distribution and are very interesting for $FMGE$.

The graphs in training, validation and test sets of the respective graph datasets were merged in order to construct datasets for graph clustering experimentation.

Clustering: We have employed the well known and popular k-means clustering paradigm with Euclidean distance and random non-deterministic initialization for our experiments. We define the number of clusters k equal to 22 in case of GREC database, 11 in case of FingerPrint dataBase and 2 for Mutagenicity database; which are actually the original number of classes in each of these datasets of IAM dataBases [23]. The clustering evaluation is defined by the quality of $FMGE$ graph clustering by the percentage of incorrectly clustered instances [23].

The two important parameters of the improved $FMGE$ are: the number of intervals and the Morgan Index level. The first parameter of $FMGE$ is the number of fuzzy intervals to be associated to each attribute. The unsupervised learning phase of $FMGE$ learns s_i fuzzy intervals for an attribute i in input collection of graphs. The parameters s_i for attribute i is independent of other attributes. It is also important to highlight here that this parameter is not necessarily same for all attributes. The second parameter is the level of Morgan

Table 2. k-means clustering on IAM datasets: validation step

FingerPrint			GREC			Mutagenicity		
Parameters		Correctly clustered	Parameters		Correctly clustered	Parameters		Correctly clustered
MI level	Max bins	instances (%)	MI level	Max bins	instances (%)	MI level	Max bins	instances (%)
4	4	40.33	8	4	70.53	8	2	52
1	6	42.32	5	8	64.63	9	2	52
2	7	43.99	2	8	63.88	1	3	52
1	8	44.42	3	7	74.82	6	2	51.6
2	5	41.22	4	8	61.22	7	2	51.6
1	5	43.88	1	5	58.55	4	3	51.6

Table 3. Quality comparison of k-means clustering in FSMFV feature space.

DataSet	FSMFV feature vector space correctly clustered graphs (%)	
	FMGE without TNF	FMGE with TNF
FingerPrint	41.52	43.87
GREC	67.13	70.54
Mutagenicity	51.82	52.33

index which is dependent on the size of the graph. It can be defined as a list of integer values $[1...p]$ with $p \leqslant P$, P is chosen based on the underlying graph database.

As shown in Table 2, we have the first column which describes the first parameter in our method *Morgan Index Level*. This parameter defines the advanced topological node feature. In second column, we present the maximum number of fuzzy bins that can be reached by one attribute during the discretization in the unsupervised learning phase. These two tables present the results of the combination of Morgan Index level and number of fuzzy bins.

The results prove that the higher Morgan Index is, the better the result we can get. The Table 3 presents the comparison between the *FMGE* method defined in [1] and the improved *FMGE* by adding topological node feature. This illustration distinguishes clearly the improvement of results that is offered by the addition of the topological node feature *TNF* to the *FMGE* approach.

To evaluate the clustering of vectors generated from graphs by *FMGE*, we use the percentage of correctly instances defined by *Weka* library as a tool of clustering evaluation [23].

We used a different discretization method while implementing *FMGE*. Thatswhy the results for the *FMGE* without *TNF* are different from the results that Luqman et al. have reported in [1].

For FingerPrint dataset, the number of correctly clustered instances increases from 41.52% to 43.87%. Moreover, for GREC and Mutagenicity datasets, the number of correctly clustered instances increases from 67.13% to 70.54% and from 51.82% to 52.33%, respectively.

We can notice that $FMGE$ method with TNF has better results. The addition of topological information to the graph embedding approach enriches the feature vector. So, the experimental results are encouraging and demonstrate the applicability of the improved $FMGE$ method to graph clustering problem.

Classification: Graph classification has been performed on IAM graphs. We employed for classification 1-NN classifier, defined in matlab. We used two different kind of metric as classifier parameter, euclidean and correlation.

We used also Support Vector Machine SVM classifier with two different kernel functions as classifier parameter, presented in the library $LIBSVM$ [25]. We operated first the train data set to build the classifier model, than we took advantage of the valid data set to choose good classifier parameters and finally we apply the classification of $FMGE$ on the test dataset.

The evaluation of classifying the $FSMFV$s was based on the recognition rate defined by a predefined function that evaluates the performance of classifier in Matlab [23].

The Tables 4 and 5 show respectively the 1-NN classification and SVM classification performance for various datasets in IAM graph database. They compare classification quality between the $FMGE$ method defined in [1] and the improved FMGE by adding topological node feature. This illustration distinguishes clearly the improvement that is offered by the addition of the topological node feature TNF to the FMGE approach.

For Fingerprint dataset, the recognition rate decreases from 64.5% to 65.5% using 1-NN with euclidean distance and from 46.32% to 47.52% with correlation. SVM classifier also presents a decreasing recognition rates comparing $FMGE$ with TNF and $FMGE$ without TNF. This decrease is a small difference defined by the order 1%. Fingerprint database contains some node features which are meaningless. For example the x/y coordinates are not discriminating enough. So, the fact that the classification results decrease while adding topological node feature to FMGE can be justified.

Table 4. Experimental results for graph 1-NN classification on IAM database.

Datasets	1-NN classifier [euclidean dist]		1-NN classifier [Correlation]	
	FMGE without TNF(%)	FMGE with TNF(%)	FMGE without TNF(%)	FMGE with TNF(%)
FingerPrint	65.5	64.5	47.52	46.32
GREC	97.34	97.72	97.53	96.58
Mutagenicity	65.98	70.47	64.52	71.76

Table 5. Experimental results for graph SVM classification on IAM database.

Datasets	SVM classifier [Gaussian Kernal]		SVM classifier [polynomial Kernal]	
	FMGE without TNF (%)	FMGE with TNF (%)	FMGE without TNF (%)	FMGE with TNF (%)
FingerPrint	69.53	69.43	69.83	68.73
GREC	50.76	50.95	95	96.39
Mutagenicity	55.37	71.33	55.41	59.35

For GREC dataset, the recognition rate increases from 97.34% to 97.72% and decreases from 97.53% to 96.58% using respectively 1-NN with euclidean distance and correlation measure. While using SVM classifier, FMGE with TNF presents a recognition rate bigger than FMGE without TNF, 96.39% bigger than 95% using polynomial kernel function parameter.

For Mutagenicity dataset, the recognition rate increases from 65.98% to 70.47% and from 64.52% to 71.76% using respectively 1-NN with euclidean distance and correlation measure. Using SVM classifier, the results increase from 55.37% to 71.33% and from 55.41% to 59.35% using respectively Gaussian kernel function and polynomial kernel as parameter of SVM.

We notice also that the recognition rates are better using, euclidean metric as classifier parameter, than using correlation metric. For example, recognition rate while classifying $FMGE$ with TNF using euclidean distance 64.5% is higher than 46.32% using correlation for Fingerprint, 97.72% is higher than 96.58% for GREC. But, for Mutagenicity, the correlation metric is better than euclidean distance, as 71.76% is bigger than 65.98%.

While using these two kinds of classifiers, we can perceive that SVM classifier provides results quiet similar to 1-NN classifier. For example, the recognition rate of $FMGE$ with TNF for Mutagenicity using 1-NN is 70.47% close to 71.33% using SVM.

The performance of $FMGE$ with more graph topological information is proved by the results of graph classification using two kind of classifiers 1-NN and SVM.

5 Conclusion

In this paper, we have presented an extension to the *Fuzzy Multilevel Graph Embedding (FMGE)* technique by adding the *Topological Node Features (TNF)*. The TNF enables $FMGE$ to encode more details on the structure and topology of the underlying graphs. As a result of the latter, the improved $FMGE$ has obtained good graph clustering and graph classification results on the *GREC*, *Mutagenicity* and *Fingerprint* graphs of the IAM graph database.

One basic discretization technique is used in this paper defined by *Discretization* filter in *Weka* library [23]. However, $FMGE$ is fully capable of employing sophisticated state-of-the-art discretization methods. Also, our proposed framework employs trapezoidal membership function from fuzzy logic but *FMGE* is fully capable of utilizing any of the available membership functions from fuzzy logic. In light of domain knowledge, appropriate choices could be made for discretization technique and fuzzy membership function.

To take this research work forward, we are working on employing the improved *FMGE* for the problem of symbol spotting and the problems of graph indexing and graph retrieval.

Acknowledgment. Hana Jarraya would like to acknowledge that the paper was conceived and largely completed during her masters at University of Tours (France), but some of the manuscript editing was done after starting her Ph.D. at Computer Vision Center (Barcelona, Spain) under supervision of Prof. Josep Lladòs Canet and Dr. Oriol Ramos Terrades.

References

1. Luqman, M.M., Ramel, J.Y., Llados, J., Brouard, T.: Fuzzy multi level graph embedding. Pattern Recogn. **46**, 551–565 (2013)
2. Lladós, J., Sánchez, G.: Symbol recognition using graphs. In: ICIP, pp. 49–52 (2003)
3. Chhabra, A.K.: Graphic symbol recognition: an overview. In: Tombre, K., Chhabra, A.K. (eds.) GREC 1997. LNCS, vol. 1389, pp. 68–79. Springer, Heidelberg (1998). doi:10.1007/3-540-64381-8_40
4. Lladós, J., Valveny, E., Sánchez, G., Martí, E.: Symbol recognition: current advances and perspectives. In: Blostein, D., Kwon, Y.-B. (eds.) GREC 2001. LNCS, vol. 2390, pp. 104–128. Springer, Heidelberg (2002). doi:10.1007/3-540-45868-9_9
5. Tombre, K., Tabbone, S., Dosch, P.: Musings on symbol recognition. In: Liu, W., Lladós, J. (eds.) GREC 2005. LNCS, vol. 3926, pp. 23–34. Springer, Heidelberg (2006). doi:10.1007/11767978_3
6. Cordella, L.P., Vento, M.: Symbol recognition in documents: a collection of techniques? IJDAR **3**(2), 73–88 (2000)
7. Jiang, X., Münger, A., Bunke, H.: Synthesis of representative graphical symbols by computing generalized median graph. In: Chhabra, A.K., Dori, D. (eds.) GREC 1999. LNCS, vol. 1941, pp. 183–192. Springer, Heidelberg (2000). doi:10.1007/3-540-40953-X_15
8. Dahma, N., Bunke, H., Caelli, T., Gao, Y.: Efficient subgraph matching using topological node feature constraints. Pattern Recogn. **48**, 317–330 (2015)
9. Wiskott, L., Fellous, J.-M., Kuiger, N., von der Malsburg, C.: Face recognition by elastic bunch graph matching. IEEE Trans. Pattern Anal. Mach. Intell. **19**, 775–779 (1997)
10. Shi, J., Malik, J.: Normalized cuts and image segmentation. IEEE Trans. Pattern Anal. Mach. Intell. **22**, 888–905 (2000)
11. Conte, D., Ramel, J.-Y., Sidère, N., Luqman, M.M., Gaüzère, B., Gibert, J., Brun, L., Vento, M.: A comparison of explicit and implicit graph embedding methods for pattern recognition. In: Kropatsch, W.G., Artner, N.M., Haxhimusa, Y., Jiang, X. (eds.) GbRPR 2013. LNCS, vol. 7877, pp. 81–90. Springer, Heidelberg (2013). doi:10.1007/978-3-642-38221-5_9
12. Bunke, H., Riesen, K.: Recent advances in graph-based pattern recognition with applications in document analysis. Pattern Recogn. **44**(5), 1057–1067 (2011)

13. Luqman, M.M., Llados, J., Ramel, J.-Y., Brouard, T.: Dimensionality reduction for fuzzy-interval based explicit graph embedding. In: Ninth IAPR International Workshop on Graphics RECognition, Séoul, South Korea, vol. 9, pp. 117–120, September 2011

14. Sidere, N., Heroux, P., Ramel, J.-Y.: Vector representation of graphs: application to the classification of symbols and letters. In: ICDAR 2009, Barcelona, Spain, pp. 681–685 (2009)

15. Luqman, M.M., Delalandre, M., Brouard, T., Ramel, J.-Y., Lladós, J.: Fuzzy intervals for designing structural signature: an application to graphic symbol recognition. In: Ogier, J.-M., Liu, W., Lladós, J. (eds.) GREC 2009. LNCS, vol. 6020, pp. 12–24. Springer, Heidelberg (2010). doi:10.1007/978-3-642-13728-0_2

16. Liwicki, M., Bunke, H., Pittman, J.A., Knerr, S.: Combining diverse systems for handwritten text line recognition. Mach. Vis. Appl. **22**, 39–51 (2011)

17. Riesen, K., Bunke, H.: IAM graph database repository for graph based pattern recognition and machine learning. In: Structural, Syntactic, and Statistical Pattern Recognition, pp. 287–297 (2008)

18. Dutta, A., Lladós, J., Bunke, H., Pal, U.: A product graph based method for dual subgraph matching applied to symbol spotting. In: Lamiroy, B., Ogier, J.-M. (eds.) GREC 2013. LNCS, vol. 8746, pp. 11–24. Springer, Heidelberg (2014). doi:10.1007/978-3-662-44854-0_2

19. Hoang Nam, H.O., Christophe, R., Jean-Christophe, B., Jean-Marc, O.: Redundant structure detection in attributed adjacency graphs for character detection in comics books. In: 10th IAPR International Workshop on Graphics Recognition, United States, August 2013

20. Rusiñol, M., Karatzas, D., Lladós, J.: Spotting graphical symbols in camera-acquired documents in real time. In: Lamiroy, B., Ogier, J.-M. (eds.) GREC 2013. LNCS, vol. 8746, pp. 3–10. Springer, Heidelberg (2014). doi:10.1007/978-3-662-44854-0_1

21. Fankhauser, S., Riesen, K., Bunke, H., Dickinson, P.: Suboptimal graph isomorphism using bipartite matching. Int. J. Pattern Recogn. Artif. Intell. **26**, 1250013 (2012)

22. Morgan, H.L.: The generation of a unique machine description for chemical structures a technique developed at chemical abstracts service. J. Chem. Doc. **5**, 107–113 (1965)

23. Arthur, D., Vassilvitskii, S.: k-means++: the advantages of carefull seeding. In: Proceedings of the Eighteenth Annual ACM-SIAM Symposium on Discrete Algorithms, pp. 1027–1035 (2007)

24. Fayyad, U.M., Irani, K.B.: Multi-interval discretization of continuous valued attributes for classification learning. In: Thirteenth International Joint Conference on Artificial Intelligence, pp. 1022–1027 (1993)

25. Fan, R.E., Chen, P.H., Lin, C.J.: Working set selection using second order information for training SVM. J. Mach. Learn. Res. **6**, 1889–1918 (2005)

Text-Independent Speech Balloon Segmentation for Comics and Manga

Christophe Rigaud$^{(\boxtimes)}$, Jean-Christophe Burie, and Jean-Marc Ogier

Laboratoire L3i, Université de La Rochelle, Avenue Michel Crépeau,
17042 La Rochelle, France
{christophe.rigaud,jcburie,jmogier}@univ-lr.fr

Abstract. Comics and manga are one of the most popular and familiar forms of graphic content over the world and play a major role in spreading country's culture. Nowadays, massive digitization and digital-born materials allow page-per-page mobile reading but we believe that other usages may be released in the near future. In this paper, we focus on speech balloon segmentation which is a key issue for text/graphic association in scanned and digital-born comic book images. Speech balloons are at the interface between text and comic characters, they inform the reader about speech tone and the position of the speakers. We present a generic and text-independent speech balloon segmentation method based on color, shape and topological organization of the connected-components. The method has been evaluated at pixel-level on two public datasets (eBDtheque and Manga109) and the F-measure results are 78.24% and 80.04% respectively.

Keywords: Graphic recognition · Speech balloon · Comics image analysis · Manga image analysis

1 Introduction

The sales of digital comics are now reaching 10% of the comics market and has doubled during the last five years[1]. Such new way of reading allows new capabilities thanks to the richness of the drawings and the recent development of mobile platform reading tools. Apart from layout re-flowing (panel re-arrangement) according to screen size, there are few work exploring other ways of reading.

In this paper, we address pixel-level balloon segmentation in order to retrieve position and shape of the speech balloons. Both information are key issues for comics understanding, especially for balloon classification [15] and comic character association [18]. This last information is not explicitly drawn by the cartoonist into the drawing but understood by the reader according to the position of the elements in the images. Speech balloons are placed in a way that helps the reader to associate them with comic characters and follow the story. Panel, balloon and comic character positions are the three information required to associate speech

---

[1] Milton Griepp's White Paper, ICv2 Conference 2014.

© Springer International Publishing AG 2017
B. Lamiroy and R. Dueire Lins (Eds.): GREC 2015, LNCS 9657, pp. 133–147, 2017.
DOI: 10.1007/978-3-319-52159-6_10

(a)   Rectangular (b) Wavy   speech (c) Oval speech bal- (d) Unusual thought
speech   balloon balloon with   tail loon with tail and balloon with tail and
with tail and gray and yellowed back- clear background   complex background
background   ground

Fig. 1. Pixel-level speech balloon segmentation results (red line) for different balloon shape and background. (Color figure online)

balloons and comic characters towards comics understanding. Panel extraction is the easiest task in comics image analysis and several studies exceed 80% recall and precision [10,20]. Balloon extraction attracted little attention even-though it is an helpful information for text extraction and essential for text/graphics association. Comic character extraction is at its early stage and the information of speech balloon positions together with their tail can be very helpful for such complex graphics extraction [18]. Pixel-level speech balloon extraction appears to be important for further processing such as balloon contour and tail analysis compared to usual bounding boxes (Fig. 1).

We propose a text-independent approach for speech balloon extraction appropriated for extracting any closed balloon (balloons with a fully connected outline, the most common type of balloon). We base our approach on the observation that speech balloons are highly contrasted region which contain aligned elements (text property). In the following, we will use the word *comics* to designate all types of comics including *Manga* (Japanese comic art).

Balloons (or bubbles) are key elements in comics, they contain most of the textual information and go pairwise with comic characters (speakers). Few works about balloon extraction have been done until now and mainly closed speech balloons have been studied. These works are based on connected-component analysis. Arai [1] proposed first a white blob detection method using four filtering rules related to manga image analysis. The rules are based on blob size, white pixel occurrences, presence of vertical spaces and width to length ratio. Later our group uses HSV color space to make a first selection of bright blobs and then consider as balloons the blobs with a ratio between the text area and the blob bounding box higher than 60% [8]. Recently, Liu [12] proposed to learn text and balloon features in order to recognize any closed speech balloons with a white background.

Open balloon extraction (balloons with partial outline) attracted little attention, a first attempt have been proposed by our team by inflating a contour around text regions [16]. Liu *et al.* proposed a systematic blob classification method (SVM) based on both shape and text properties (two for each) [11]. Both approaches require text positions as input.

Section 2 presents the proposed speech balloon segmentation method. Section 3 the experiments we performed. Finally, Sects. 4 and 5 discuss and conclude this work respectively.

2   Speech Balloon Extraction

From the five approaches reviewed in Sect. 1, the first approach have been developed especially for manga and therefore has several weaknesses for other types of comics [1]. First, the extraction of the connected-components (CC) requires a binary image which is obtained by using a global threshold. This constraint limits its application to images with a clear background color (which tends to white). Second, balloon candidates selection is performed using several heuristics which are not validated and specific to manga. The method proposed by Ho [8] can be very efficient for a particular comics type but the set of parameter makes it not adaptive to all styles of comics and manga (e.g. heuristic of minimum percentage of text inside balloons). Liu *et al.* method achieve very high quality results but it requires speech balloons with a white background (fixed binarization threshold) and it is dependent of the training set (supervised). The two works concerning open balloon extraction requires text positions as input which is a strong constraint because of error propagation issue (from text extraction), but have the advantage to retrieve closed balloons as well [11, 16].

We propose to overcome these limitations by using an unsupervised method based on adaptive thresholding in order to first binarize the gray-level image, extract and then analyze the connected-components. The advantage of using a local and adaptive threshold selection method for comics segmentation has already been demonstrated in our previous work [17]. As for document image analysis in general, it limits original strokes to be broken (Fig. 2). After having extracted all the CC, we select only the ones with a particular color, topology and shape, independently from size and script (written signs) and compute an overall confidence value that is used for the final speech balloon/non-speech balloon classification.

2.1   Adaptive Threshold Selection

During comics or manga creation process, balloon outlines are first drawn using a black stroke and then filled with text [4]. We propose to rely on these two information which are intrinsic to their design process and thus characteristics of speech balloons.

Speech balloon outlines are intentionally created in a continuous way by the artist whether they are straight or curved (single stroke). Sometimes, they appear to be degraded when reaching the final reader due to image digitization or compression. A perfect outline segmentation and connected-component extraction would result in one single connected-component per balloon outline (Fig. 2).

Fig. 2. Binarization results of a 8 bits gray image at different threshold levels from the lower (top-left) to the higher (bottom-right) with threshold 50, 100, 150, 200. We observe that the black strokes are broken at a low threshold level and the background starts to appear as salt and paper noise due to paper texture at high threshold value [17]. The best binarization corresponds to threshold 150 in this example. Images credits: [19].

However, complex background regions complicate this step. There are several adaptive threshold selection method in the literature [9], however, speech balloon being a highly contrasted region it facilitates the separation of background (usually white) and content (black text) in this region. The main difficulties are the shape and the size of the sliding window which is used to determine if a pixel belongs to the background or foreground for each local regions. Having no *a priori* information about speech balloon location, shape and size, we define a squared window of size *blockSize* relative to the image size. We define the threshold value $T(x, y)$ as the mean of the squared $blockSize * blockSize$ neighborhood of (x, y). The corresponding pixel at position (x, y) is considered as part of the foreground if its gray-value is above T or background else. Figure 3 shows binarization results of comics and manga from different nature and definition using this approach.

After image thresholding, we obtain a binary image from which we extract and analyze the relationship between white and black connected-components (CC) using a connected-component labeling algorithm proposed by Suzuki [21]. The CC are split into two sets according to their color in order to ease further

(a) Recent French comics (A4 page digitized at 300DPI)
(b) Old French comics (A4 page digitized at 300DPI)
(c) Recent manga (digital-born with JPEG compression 150DPI)
(d) Golden age American comics (A4 page digitized at 300DPI)

Fig. 3. Binarization results of comics and manga from different nature and definition. Original images are in Fig. 1.

processing (speech balloon outline/content separation). White and black sets are called W and B respectively. Note that other region extraction techniques (e.g. MSER [5]) could be used but an extra processing should be added as we also need the topological relations.

2.2 Balloon Candidate Selection

As introduced earlier, speech balloons can be seen as speech text containers which involves text to be inside speech balloons. From a topological point of view, the first region including speech balloon content (text) is speech balloon background (e.g. white region surrounded by a black outline). Note that balloon background regions are assumed to be part of set W because there are usually brighter than their content (part of set B). We propose to combine color and topological feature for selecting from the set W, only the CC (parents) containing other CC (children) which are part of set B. We call this subset of parents the "balloon candidates" CC (Fig. 4). Note that the biggest white CC, which usually corresponds to image background, is ignored as well as very small regions (whose size is lower than 0.5% of image size) usually caused by paper texture or image compression region binarisation.

In the next subsection, shape and spatial organization of each balloon candidates are analyzed in order to determine if it contains text-like information (CC which are aligned).

2.3 Balloon Candidate Analysis

We propose to analyze the content organization of each balloon candidate in order to determine if it contains speech text-like information (assuming speech balloons contain speech text). Speech text has several characteristics, some from the text domain and other from comics domain. Text information has some

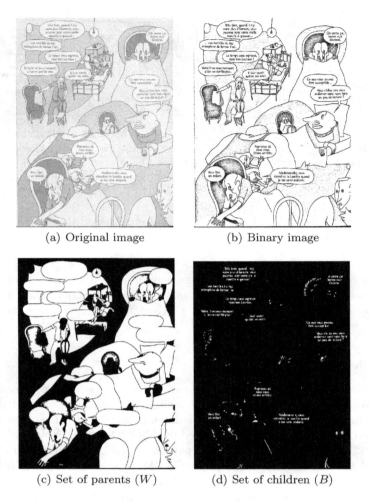

(a) Original image   (b) Binary image

(c) Set of parents (*W*)   (d) Set of children (*B*)

Fig. 4. Sets of balloon candidate (*W*) and theirs content (*B*) for a given image. Corresponding CC are represented in white for both sets. Image credits: [19].

characteristics which are language independent like alignment and equally separated glyphs with noticeable contrast to their background, constant stroke width (thickness), similar color and sizes [2]. When text is used for speech in comics, it is most of the time aligned and centered inside a bubble-like region but glyph space and stroke width are not always stable because text may be handwritten. The difficulty for comics analysis is the important amount of graphics that also consist of aligned elements and confuses balloon/non-balloon separation process (e.g. roofing tile, grass, hairs and face). Such graphics could be disguarded by using an OCR system but currently, commercial OCR systems are not accurate enough for many handwritten comic fonts.

In the following approach, we combine inside balloon CC alignment and balloon shape to compute a confidence value for each balloon candidate. The confidence value is used for the final balloon/non-balloon candidate decision (Sect. 3).

Content alignment. The children are supposed to be horizontally or vertically aligned according to the language (e.g. vertical for Japanese, horizontal for English or French). This is a characteristic of speech text in comics and also for text in general. We propose to "scan" each candidate content and compute the percentage of children which are aligned called inter-child alignment value (*cAlign*). The scanning direction (top-to-bottom or left-to-right) is defined manually here for simplifying but it could be defined automatically by applying both direction separately and then select the one that provides the best results (Sect. 2.3).

We compute the percentage of aligned children in a specific order, from the longest to the shortest line of aligned children in order to find the longest lines first (the most representative of text-like information). Two children are considered as horizontally aligned if the center of one of them passes through the other. For instance, for two children A and B and their respective center (cx, cy), B is horizontally aligned to A if $A.ymin < B.cy < A.ymax$. Similarly, vertical alignment is computed by replacing y by x. Note that three children minimum are required to compute a relevant alignment.

The process stops automatically when there is less remaining non-aligned children than the number of lines already found. In this manner, we ignore non-aligned children corresponding to punctuations, accents, disconnected-components, etc. (Fig. 5).

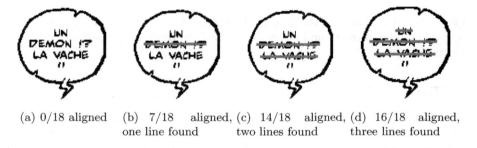

(a) 0/18 aligned   (b) 7/18 aligned, one line found   (c) 14/18 aligned, two lines found   (d) 16/18 aligned, three lines found

Fig. 5. Children CC alignment scanning process. The process stops automatically when there is less remaining CC than discovered lines (e.g. in sub-figure 5(d), three lines have been discovered and only two children are remaining).

Shape analysis. Speech balloon shape is similar to a bubble that contains elements (mainly text). It is usually bounded by an outline stroke that has some irregularities throughout its perimeter, the two biggest ones being in the region of the tail [14]. We propose to measure the overall convexity of the outline in order to find how similar to a perfect bubble the balloon candidate is. Several measures of convex polygon exist in the literature [3], some are based on area and others on perimeter analysis. We select a perimeter based approach as it is the most deformable part of the shape. The convexity measure (*cShape*) is defined as the ratio between the Euclidean perimeter of the convex hull of the measured shape S and the Euclidean perimeter of the measured shape (Eq. 1).

$$cShape = \frac{arcLength(hull(S))}{arcLength(S)} \tag{1}$$

Note that the convexity measure is equal to 100% for perfect rectangles, squares, ovals, circles etc. This could be the case for speech balloon without tail but not for the others because tail region is usually non convex in order to be easily distinguishable. However, tail perimeter is small compared to the overall perimeter of a speech balloon and has a minor impact on the proposed convexity measure. Tail regions could be detected and removed using a tail detection approach [14] but we have preferred to avoid error propagation issue in this process and decided do not use it.

Confidence value. The global confidence value C is computed for each balloon candidate, from inter-child alignment *cAlign* and shape *cShape* measures according to Formula 2.

$$C = cAlign * \alpha + cShape * \beta \tag{2}$$

where α and β are two weighting parameters defined experimentally (Sect. 3.2).

3   Experiments

In this section we evaluate the proposed method of speech balloon segmentation using two public datasets and compare our results to other approaches from the literature.

3.1   Datasets

We evaluate the proposed method using the two public datasets eBDtheque [7] and Manga109 [13] in order to show the robustness of the proposed method for French comics, English comics and Japanese manga (script independence evaluation).

The eBDtheque dataset was designed to be as representative as possible of the comics diversity, it includes few pages of diverse albums. It is composed by one hundred images which are composed by 850 panels, 1550 comics characters, 1092 balloons (84.5% are closed) and 4691 text lines. It contains images scanned from French comic books (46%), French webcomics (37%) with various formats and definitions, public domain American comics (11%) and unpublished artwork of manga (6%). In addition to the diversity of styles, formats and definitions, there are also differences in design and printing techniques since 29% of the images were published before 1953 and 71% after 2000. This dataset provides pixel-level object regions as part of the groundtruth.

Manga109 dataset is a selection of 109 manga titles published from the 1970s to the 2010s (21142 images in total). They have been selected from the archive "Manga Library Z" run by J-comi[2]. "*The Manga109 dataset covers various kinds of categories, including humor, battle, romantic comedy, animal, science fiction, sports, historical drama, fantasy, love, romance, suspense, horror, and four-frame cartoons*" [13]. Only text transcription of four titles is publicly available as groundtruth but the authors provide groundtruthing tools. This dataset being quite huge, pixel-level speech balloon groundtruth creation would require a lot of time. We preferred to select few titles and manually count the number of correct/incorrect/missed speech balloons in each image. We randomly selected a subset of three titles that represent 408 images and 3242 balloons in total ("Momoyama Haikagura", "Tetsu San" and "Ultra Eleven").

3.2   Confidence Value Validation

The two measures proposed in Sect. 2.3 have been evaluated separately and combined in order to define the best weighting parameters α and β from Formula 2 (see Fig. 6). The best performance has been achieved for $\alpha = 0.75$ and $\beta = 0.25$.

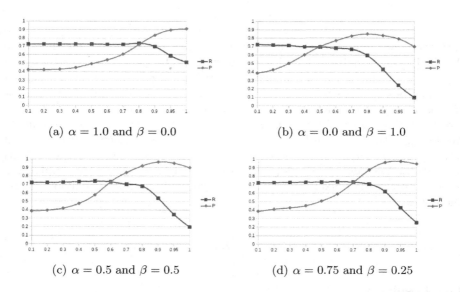

(a) $\alpha = 1.0$ and $\beta = 0.0$ (b) $\alpha = 0.0$ and $\beta = 1.0$

(c) $\alpha = 0.5$ and $\beta = 0.5$ (d) $\alpha = 0.75$ and $\beta = 0.25$

Fig. 6. Confidence value weighting parameter validation (α and β). Vertical axis represents the percentage of recall R and precision P while the horizontal axis is the minimum confidence required for a balloon to be considered as true positive.

---

[2] http://www.j-comi.jp/.

3.3   Performance Evaluation

We evaluate the performance of the proposed method at pixel-level and bounding box level for eBDtheque dataset in order to give both precise and comparable results with other methods from the literature providing only bounding box level results. However, the results over the Manga109 subset have only been evaluated visually at object level because of the lack of speech balloon position information in the provided groundtruth. The latter has been performed for speech balloon candidates with a minimum confidence value $C \geq 80\%$ in order to evaluate the performance of the 20% best results provided by the proposed method. Concerning adaptive threshold selection, the *blockSize* was defined as a square of area 1.3% of the image area according to the validation on the eBDtheque dataset [7].

For pixel-level evaluation, balloon candidates pixels were considered true positives TP if they were corresponding to a balloon pixel in the groundtruth or false positives FP. The number of TP, FP and false negative (missed pixels) FN were used to compute the recall R and the precision P of each of the methods using Formulas 3 and 4. We also computed the F-measure F for each result.

$$R = \frac{TP}{TP + FN} \tag{3}$$

$$P = \frac{TP}{TP + FP} \tag{4}$$

Concerning bounding box level evaluation, we use the same metric as the PASCAL VOC challenge for visual objects [6]. The detections were assigned to ground truth objects and judged to be true or false positives by measuring bounding box overlaps between detected and groundtruth regions. To be considered as a correct detection, the overlap ratio a_0 between the predicted bounding box B_p and the ground truth bounding box B_{gt} must exceed 0.5 (Formula 5). According to the PASCAL VOC challenge, the predicted objects were considered as true positive TP if $a_0 > 0.5$ or false positive FP otherwise. Missed balloons were counted as false negatives (FN). Note that bounding box level evaluation is less accurate than pixel-level evaluation, especially for speech balloon having a long tail (Fig. 7).

$$a_0 = \frac{area(B_p \cap B_{gt})}{area(B_p \cup B_{gt})} \tag{5}$$

3.4   Results Analysis

For the first dataset (eBDtheque), we compared the proposed method to other methods from the literature at pixel and bounding box (BdB) levels. Result details are given Table 1. Note that Liu *et al.* [11] reported results at bounding box level only and using a slightly stricter ratio ($a_0 > 0.6$).

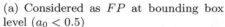

(a) Considered as FP at bounding box level ($a_0 < 0.5$)

(b) Considered as TP at pixel level ($>$ 90% pixels match)

Fig. 7. Difference of performance evaluation results for a same balloon extraction using bounding box level groundtruth (left) and pixel level groundtruth (right). Red and blue polygons correspond to detection and groundtruth regions respectively. (Color figure online)

At pixel level, the proposed method provides the best results compared to other method from the literature, including a method proposed by our team which uses a simplified scenario by requiring text positions as input [16]. The recall of 70.71% has been measured over all eBDtheque dataset which contains 15.5% of open balloons (non detectable by the proposed approach). The remaining 13.79% of errors are due to small balloons containing few information or graphics (Fig. 8(a)). The regions that confuse the proposed approach (drop of precision) are often composed by illustrative text or text-like elements (Fig. 8(d) and (e)).

Concerning bounding box level evaluation, the proposed approach exceeds our previous approach [16] but not the state of the art methods [11]. Nevertheless, the proposed method has the advantage do not require text position as input.

Concerning the Manga109 dataset subset, we report an average performance of the proposed method for recall, precision and F-measure of 72.24%, 89.71% and 80.04% (see Table 2). The overall performance is similar to eBDtheque

Table 1. Average speech balloon segmentation performance in percent for eBDtheque.

	eBDtheque dataset					
	Pixel level			BdB level		
Method	R	P	F_1	R	P	F_1
Arai [1]	18.70	23.14	20.69	13.40	11.76	12.53
Ho [8]	14.78	32.37	20.30	13.96	24.76	17.84
Rigaud [16]	69.81	32.83	44.66	52.68	44.17	48.05
Liu [11]	–	–	–	**90.10**	**86.90**	**88.50**
Proposed	**70.71**	**87.62**	**78.24**	72.21	83.31	77.36

Table 2. Average speech balloon segmentation performance in percent for Manga109.

| | Manga109 dataset | | |
| | Pixel level | | |
Method	R	P	F_1
Proposed	72.24	89.71	80.04

dataset which confirms that the proposed method is non sensitive to comics style variations (comics vs manga). The same limits as eBDtheque dataset have been observed: recall and precision drops are mainly due to open balloons (Fig. 8(b)) and illustrative text in balloon like regions (Fig. 8(f)).

More detailed results and extra material are available on GitHub[3].

(a) Less than three aligned element are inside the balloon (two only)

(b) Open balloons not detected by the proposed method

(c) Outline-free balloon not detected by the proposed method

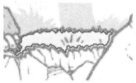

(d) Grass is aligned as text in an balloon-like region

(e) Illustration containing text (truck cover)

(f) Illustration containing text (blackboard)

Fig. 8. Examples of failure cases of the proposed approach that drops down recall on the first row (FN) and precision on the second row (FP). Detected balloons are represented by a red line in the second row. (Color figure online)

---

[3] https://github.com/crigaud/publication/tree/master/2016/LNCS/
text-independent_speech_balloon_segmentation_for_comics_and_manga.

4   Discussion

The proposed method uses a simple adaptive thresholding approach which is efficient for the studied scope because speech balloon regions are composed by a background which is easy to binarize when taken apart from the rest of the image (local thresholding). Note that the proposed approach assumes speech balloon background to be brighter than their content, if this is not the case, image color inversion should be applied before binarizing. Speech balloon candidate selection is based on content analysis which sometimes ends up with false positives because other graphics have a similar-to-text organization. Open balloons can be included into this approach by analyzing page background content (contains open balloon text). Note that the presented approach provides balloon background regions (white regions) but some processing require balloon outline (e.g. tail direction retrieval). In such situation, the proposed results have to be post-processed in order to find the external edge of the outline stroke like [12]. This work focus on comics analysis but we believe it can also be applied on other images having strong relations between text and graphic shapes such as engineering flowchart, car plates and road signs.

5   Conclusion

This paper presents an unsupervised speech balloon segmentation approach toward comics and manga text/graphic association. The proposed method combines color, shape and topological connected-component relationship analysis in order to segment speech balloon contours at the level of pixels. We also proposed a segmentation confidence measure mixing speech balloon content and shape which can be useful for several applications. The proposed approach has been tested over most of the comics types with promising performance from two public datasets eBDtheque [7] and Manga109 [13]. In the future, we will include open balloons segmentation in the method.

Acknowledgment. This work was supported by the University of La Rochelle (France), the town of La Rochelle and the PIA-iiBD ("Programme d'Investissements d'Avenir"). We are grateful to all authors and publishers of comics and manga images from eBDtheque and Manga109 datasets for allowing us to use their works.

References

1. Arai, K., Tolle, H.: Method for real time text extraction of digital manga comic. Int. J. Image Process. (IJIP) 4(6), 669–676 (2011)
2. Bigorda, L.G., Karatzas, D.: A fast hierarchical method for multi-script and arbitrary oriented scene text extraction. CoRR abs/1407.7504 (2014). http://arxiv.org/abs/1407.7504
3. Chalmeta, R., Hurtado, F., Sacristn, V., Saumell, M.: Measuring regularity of convex polygons. Comput. Aided Des. 45(2), 93–104 (2013). http://www.sciencedirect.com/science/article/pii/S0010448512001650. Solid and Physical Modeling 2012

4. Cyb: Making Comics: Storytelling Secrets of Comics, Manga and Graphic Novels, pp. 128–153. William Morrow Paperbacks (2006)
5. Donoser, M., Bischof, H.: Efficient maximally stable extremal region (MSER) tracking. In: 2006 IEEE Computer Society Conference on Computer Vision and Pattern Recognition, vol. 1, pp. 553–560. IEEE (2006)
6. Everingham, M., Van Gool, L., Williams, C.K., Winn, J., Zisserman, A.: The pascal visual object classes (VOC) challenge. Int. J. Comput. Vision **88**(2), 303–338 (2010)
7. Guérin, C., Rigaud, C., Mercier, A., et al.: eBDtheque: a representative database of comics. In: Proceedings of International Conference on Document Analysis and Recognition (ICDAR), pp. 1145–1149. Washington DC (2013)
8. Ho, A.K.N., Burie, J.C., Ogier, J.M.: Panel and speech balloon extraction from comic books. In: 10th IAPR International Workshop on Document Analysis Systems, pp. 424–428, March 2012
9. Lamiroy, B., Ogier, J.M.: Analysis and interpretation of graphical documents. In: Doermann, D., Tombre, K. (eds.) Handbook of Document Image Processing and Recognition. Springer, London (2014). doi:10.1007/978-0-85729-859-1_19
10. Li, L., Wang, Y., Suen, C.Y., Tang, Z., Liu, D.: A tree conditional random field model for panel detection in comic images. Pattern Recogn. **48**(7), 2129–2140 (2015). http://dx.doi.org/10.1016/j.patcog.2015.01.011
11. Liu, X., Wang, Y., Tang, Z.: A clump splitting based method to localize speech balloons in comics. In: Proceedings of the 13th International Conference on Document Analysis and Recognition (ICDAR), pp. 901–906. IEEE (2015)
12. Liu, X., Li, C., Zhu, H., Wong, T.T., Xu, X.: Text-aware balloon extraction from manga. Vis. Comput. **32**(4), 501–511 (2015). http://dx.doi.org/10.1007/s00371-015-1084-0
13. Matsui, Y., Ito, K., Aramaki, Y., Yamasaki, T., Aizawa, K.: Sketch-based manga retrieval using manga109 dataset. CoRR abs/1510.04389 (2015). http://arxiv.org/abs/1510.04389
14. Rigaud, C., Guérin, C., Karatzas, D., Burie, J.C., Ogier, J.M.: Knowledge-driven understanding of images in comic books. Int. J. Doc. Anal. Recogn. (IJDAR) **18**(3), 199–221 (2015). http://dx.doi.org/10.1007/s10032-015-0243-1
15. Rigaud, C., Karatzas, D., Burie, J.-C., Ogier, J.-M.: Adaptive contour classification of comics speech balloons. In: Lamiroy, B., Ogier, J.-M. (eds.) GREC 2013. LNCS, vol. 8746, pp. 53–62. Springer, Heidelberg (2014). doi:10.1007/978-3-662-44854-0_5
16. Rigaud, C., Karatzas, D., Van de Weijer, J., Burie, J.C., Ogier, J.M.: An active contour model for speech balloon detection in comics. In: Proceedings of the 12th International Conference on Document Analysis and Recognition (ICDAR), pp. 1240–1244. IEEE (2013)
17. Rigaud, C., Karatzas, D., Van de Weijer, J., Burie, J.C., Ogier, J.M.: Automatic text localisation in scanned comic books. In: Proceedings of the 8th International Conference on Computer Vision Theory and Applications (VISAPP). SCITEPRESS Digital Library (2013)
18. Rigaud, C., Le Thanh, N., Burie, J.C., Ogier, J.M., Iwata, M., Imazu, E., Koichi, K.: Speech balloon and speaker association for comics and manga understanding. In: Proceedings of the 13th International Conference on Document Analysis and Recognition (ICDAR), pp. 351–356. IEEE (2015)
19. Roudier, N.: Les terres creusées, volume Acte sur BD, Actes Sud (2011)

20. Stommel, M., Merhej, L.I., Müller, M.G.: Segmentation-free detection of comic panels. In: Bolc, L., Tadeusiewicz, R., Chmielewski, L.J., Wojciechowski, K. (eds.) ICCVG 2012. LNCS, vol. 7594, pp. 633–640. Springer, Heidelberg (2012). doi:10. 1007/978-3-642-33564-8_76

21. Suzuki, S., et al.: Topological structural analysis of digitized binary images by border following. Comput. Vis. Graph. Image Process. **30**(1), 32–46 (1985)

Author Index

Agarwal, Shubham   60
Agrawal, Mohit   60
Althoff, Klaus-Dieter   47

Barney Smith, Elisa H.   3
Bayer, Johannes   47
Bukhari, Syed Saqib   47
Burie, Jean-Christophe   133

Chaudhury, Santanu   60
Coustaty, Mickael   86

de las Heras, Lluís-Pere   75
Dengel, Andreas   47
Drevin, Günther   19

Fornés, Alicia   103

Jarraya, Hana   117

Lamiroy, Bart   3, 31
Langenhan, Christoph   47

Le Viet, Phuong   86
Liwicki, Marcus   47
Lladós, Josep   75, 103
Luqman, Muhammad Muzzamil   86, 117

Mattana, Vincent   19

Ogier, Jean-Marc   86, 133

Petzold, Frank   47
Pierrot, Pascal   31

Quoc Dang, Bao   86

Ramel, Jean-Yves   117
Ramos Terrades, Oriol   75
Riba, Pau   103
Rigaud, Christophe   133
Roux, Pierre   19

Tran Cao, De   86

Printed in the United States
By Bookmasters